One Down, One Dead

One Down, One Dead

The personal adventures of two Fourth Fighter Group combat pilots as they face the Luftwaffe over Germany

Frank Speer

Copyright © 2003 by Frank Speer.

Library of Congress Number: 2003091324
ISBN :   Hardcover   1-4010-9907-6
              Softcover   1-4010-9906-8

All rights reserved. No part of this book may be reproduced or transmitted in any form or by any means, electronic or mechanical, including photocopying, recording, or by any information storage and retrieval system, without permission in writing from the copyright owner.

This book was printed in the United States of America.

To order additional copies of this book, contact:
Xlibris Corporation
1-888-795-4274
www.Xlibris.com
Orders@Xlibris.com
18174-SPEE

Acknowledgement

In the early 1940s, a youth, too young to be in the military service of his country in WWII, nevertheless was enthralled by its mystery and high-speed action. He lived in the small town of Saffron Walden, Essex, England. Nearby was a combat fighter-plane complex called Debden Airbase. At every opportunity, he would mount his trusty bicycle and pedal over to the airbase. He would sit at the boundary fence watching the planes take off on their daily missions to fight the Luftwaffe or to guard the ships in the huge convoys bringing supplies to the British in their war effort.

He would count the planes as they took off, and compare the number to those that returned; often a somewhat diminished number. All of his observations were faithfully recorded in a small notebook. At first there were Hurricanes and Spitfires, flown by British pilots under British control, and later they were joined by men of different nationalities such as Polish, Canadian and American. The ground crews were primarily British WAAFs.

Later the United States became engaged in the war and the base was turned over to The U.S. Army Air Corps. The U.S. citizens in the British Air Force were then invited to become American pilots and became known as the Eagle Squadrons. At first they continued to fly Spitfires with the same WAAF crews. As time went on, the Spitfires were replaced with American P-47 Thunderbolts and the WAAF crews were replaced by American soldiers. Next, the P-47s were replaced by P-51 Mustangs with souped-up Rolls-Royce "Merlin" engines.

All was duly recorded by this youth named Keith Braybrooke.

Keith has kept up with his chronology of the Base until this very day. Who else would know more about the history of the Debden Airbase than he? Keith eventually became a professional proof-reader, and in this capacity I asked him to proof-read "One Down-One Dead." At this point I discovered how different the English and American languages are. Nevertheless, we settled our differences amicably and the resulting manuscript is now before you. I owe a debt of gratitude to Keith for his excellent work.

Before Keith ever saw the unproofed manuscript, it had to pass the critique of my dear companion Anne Kramer. Anne spent more than 30 years of her working career composing letters and polishing speeches as assistant to the president of a liberal arts college. This background made her perfect for the job of critiquing this book. She was merciless in correcting my punctuation and sentence construction, often forcing revision of entire paragraphs. No appeal would prevail, and I grudgingly acknowledge that "One Down-One Dead" is much the better for her talented hand.

In addition, when I thought the book was finished, Anne said, "Do your readers know how your flight training was accomplished? I think that story would be interesting." I immediately liked the idea, and had a good time recalling some of the more whimsical aspects of our Cadet life. A new chapter was soon born but it did not fit into the book's progression so a prolog was added; again, thanks to Anne!

A particularly difficult part of writing One Down-One Dead, was getting Mike Sobanski's diary (written in 1940s Polish) translated into English. Contemporary Polish contacts found the language too difficult. Fortunately, I finally met Maria Styczynska, PH.D. who not only was able to translate, but was eager to apply her talents to the task. She painstakingly pursued the task (nearly 400 pages) until it was completed. She enjoyed the chain of trials and tribulations, romances, and nuances of Mike's training in Canada; and she accomplished this translation while working full-time as a quality-control manager of a metallurgical company, a mother, and an avid painter. Maria has made an immeasurable contribution to this book.

Dr. Doug Cameron, a computer wizard, was extremely helpful in taking my pictures, (many somewhat worn from years of abuse), converting them into tiny little pixels and arranging them into units on a CD that miraculously translated into viewable pictures which grace this book. Dr. Doug's efforts are a real asset to One Down, One Dead.

Finally, I owe a debt of gratitude to Tim Kirkup, who found and acquired the original Sobanski diary; and to Bruce Zigler, and Tom Lowery, for their encouragement and their help in providing pictures, information, and advice. Thanks fellows, I appreciate your help. You do not write a book alone!

PROLOG

Aviation cadets
(THE WAY IT WAS)

As far back as I can remember I wanted to fly, though the possibility was quite remote. Whenever a plane passed over our farm, I would stand there in my overalls and bare feet, present task forgotten; my face tilted to the sky, and watch it until it disappeared from sight. I visualized myself at the controls, master of the universe! It took a war to provide the opportunity for me to realize my dream, but when the call went out I was in the front of the line.

The road to becoming a fighter pilot in WWII was beset with many obstacles. To be eligible, a candidate had to be old enough to enlist, be in generally good health, single, have all of his own teeth, and a college degree. With these basics he could then apply to become an Aviation Cadet, and if his application were accepted, he would be put on hold pending an opening in the training schedule-a wait of possibly six months to a year.

As the demand for pilots increased and the training facilities became available, gradually some of the prerequisites were waived in order to ensure an adequate supply of pilots for the rigors of combat. I waited patiently as they dropped the requirement for all your teeth, and despite two missing wisdom teeth that obstacle was passed. Next marriage was determined to have no bearing on a pilot's capabilities so I no longer had to contemplate the need for an annulment. Since I had been an "A" student in high school and was well-read, I had no problem passing the exhaustive two-year college-equivalency test which had by then replaced the college-degree requirement. Finally, I passed the usual "if you can walk in, have an audible heartbeat, turn your head and cough, you're in" physical, and I immediately signed up. I was then placed in the Enlisted Reserve to await a training opening.

A 1942 Eastern Pennsylvania recruiting drive rounded up 1907 of us Aviation Cadet applicants who met or exceeded these requirements. Subsequent testing reduced the number to 610, who finally were shipped by train to San Antonio Aviation Cadet Center, commonly referred to as "Sack," for further classification. The base covered hundreds of acres of what formerly was a vast semi-arid mesquite thicket at least nine miles from any semblance of civilization. There we received our clothing issue, a $10,000 Government Insurance Policy, and with a new hairstyle, "the Kelly Klip," we took on the outward appearance of soldiers.

Here our pilot aspirants' ranks were again diminished severely as further testing separated those better qualified for other duties such as bombardier, navigator, gunner or ground crew. This was accomplished by a physical examination called a "64," even more demanding than the West Point physical; psychological testing by doctors who seemed to be somewhat less than normal themselves, and finally, psycho-motor tests. I remember one well—trying to keep an electrified lance in position on a small circle moving in an eccentric path on a rapidly spinning turntable about the size of a "78" record. Meanwhile, simulated gunfire and shouts were blasted in your ears and any digression of the lance from the metal disk prompted raucous buzzing noises. To say the least, it was very stressful.

Thus classified, those remaining pilot hopefuls moved across the street to the Preflight School. Here we were to learn many new and unusual things, assisted by a cadre of upperclassmen who were most helpful in our further training. It was obvious they had been trained by experts in harassment, and it seemed they never slept. They introduced us to new ways to awake, attend to our personal hygiene, eat, dress, march, and memorize. Indeed there was very little of our civilian lifestyle and habits that did not need to be restructured in order for us to be properly prepared to engage the enemy in combat.

A course in "precision bed making" taught us how a simple task can be made complex calling for "precision and planning." The end result was a bunk assembled in a manner that made it appropriately responsive to a coin casually tossed upon it. Wall locker management also came under close scrutiny and woe to any cadet whose handkerchief encroached upon the space designated for his shorts in his locker. Each type of clothing had a specific space (in increments of 4") and place on a designated shelf. If a cadet's shoes had a speck of dust marring their mirror-like polish, a demerit invariably resulted. It seemed that shoes had to have a reflective polish at all times, in spite of the fact that the ground was either wet with mud of a chewing-gum consistency or dry with blowing dust having almost magnetic tendencies to stick to anything meant to be dust-free. It has been said that this is the only place on earth where you could be confronted with a cold blustery snowstorm and upon entering the barracks, discover gooey mud on your *dusty* shoes.

We had to be taught a proper way to eat our meals-silent, square, at attention, while sitting on only the first four inches of the front of the chair. No one ever questioned what the rest of the chair seat was designated to hold. It apparently had to do with the administration's fixation on the increments of four inches which governed all sorts of specifications such as the clothing space allocations. We learned that while seated at the table to eat "in a gentlemanly manner," hands and arms were never to touch the table. Food was always passed clockwise initially-refills passed counterclockwise. Particular attention was paid to the plate and the utensils, especially when finished eating. They were placed on the plate, in order, parallel to an invisible line running from 4 o'clock to 10 o'clock while the cadet maintained a silent position of attention until dismissed.

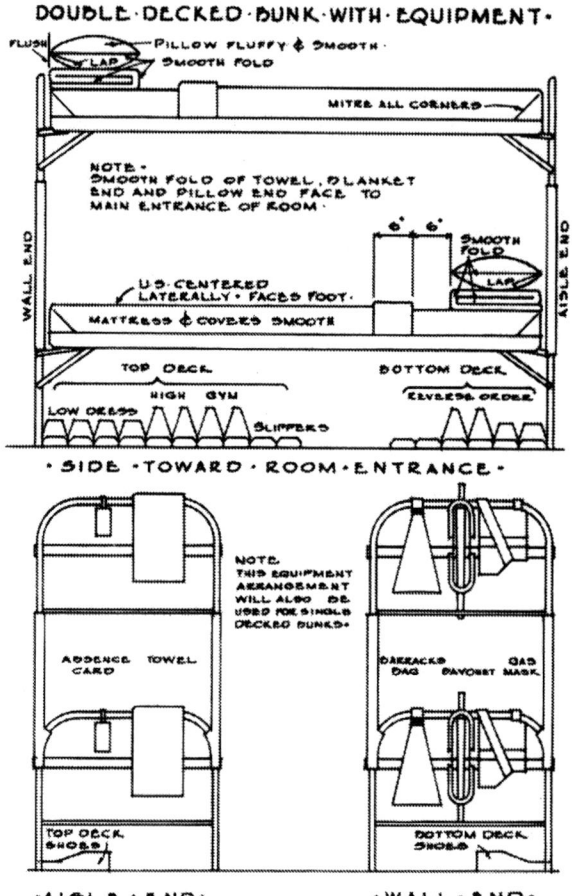

"Precision Bed Making"- An Aviation Cadet Manual prescribes in minute detail the proper way to make a bed. When finished, a coin tossed on the bed should bounce and flip due to the tension of the covers.

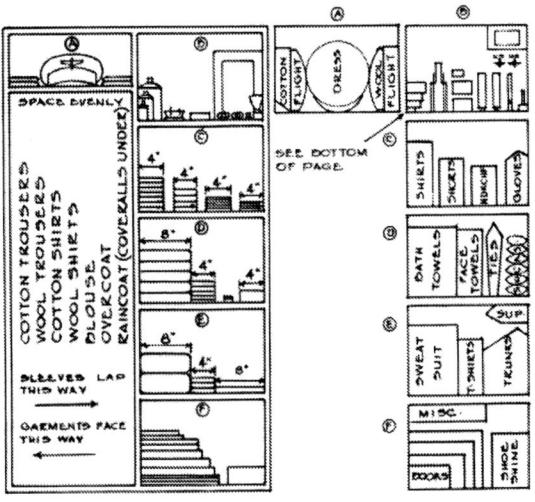

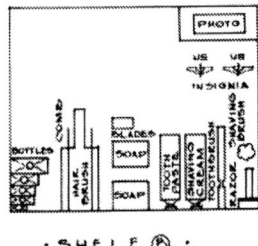

The Cadet Manual defines space allocations for each item of clothing and personal item of allowed possessions.

MESS HALL

A. Enter and leave marching at attention (2)
B. Lift, do not slide, chairs when sitting or rising (1)
C. Eat "at ease", talk only to ask for food (1)
D. Sit only on first four inches of seat (1)
E. Arms or hands never touch table or lap (1)
F. Knife, when not in use, shall be at 1200 o'clock position on plate from 1100 to 1300 (1)
G. No bridges of utensils from plate to table (1)
H. When finished, arrange utensils as below (2) and sit at attention (2)
I. On rising, napkin shall be folded once and laid across back of chair or seat of stool (1)
J. On clearing door of mess hall when leaving, double time to flight (2) and fall in at attention (2)
K. Food initially will be passed clockwise around table (1) refills counter-clockwise (1)

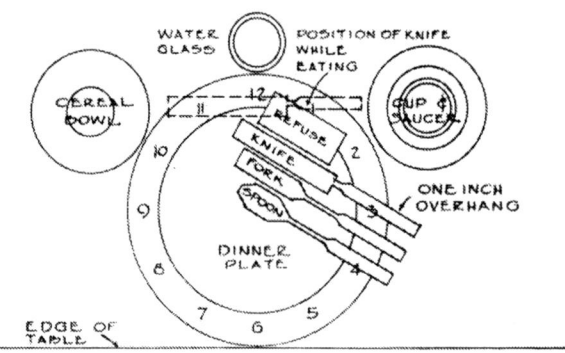

DRESSING OF UTENSILS
AT END OF MEAL

The Cadet Manual details the "Gentlemanly" approach to Aviation Cadet dining.

Outdoors there was never to be a *walking* moment – it was double-time everywhere, even though when you reached your destination, you generally had to wait. Fortunately, this gave the cadet time to catch his breath and, no matter what the weather, make sure that his shoes were clean and dust-free. (This was generally accomplished by rubbing the front and top of each shoe on the back of the opposite pants leg).

Concurrently, while learning all of these social graces, the cadet had a full agenda of academic courses, physical training (PT), and countless hours of instruction by resident upperclassmen. They made sure that every available moment was filled with cramming of information such as memorizing the "chain of command," your General Orders, military ranks, etc. No stone was left unturned to make sure you had no peaceful moments to engage in idleness. Of course, the knowledge of military ranks was useful, primarily in determining who you must salute, since as civilians, most of us had not the vaguest idea of who should rate a salute. Consequently we found the only safe practice was to salute everyone who wore a military uniform, be he private or general. This practice led to occasional amusing incidents where some new recruit using the same philosophy would throw one of us a salute, thus reaffirming that old military axiom "If it moves salute it; if it doesn't move paint it."

Leisurely days were a thing of the past. In fact, any cadet having a problem with an academic lesson would most likely find the necessary study time after taps by pulling his blanket over his head to study by flashlight, after lights out. In order to assure that we had no leisure we were given extensive training in PT, with long runs in the country in blazing hot weather, where we could observe the local flora and fauna struggling to live in the ankle-deep sand. They also gave us extensive training in "short order drill." Just to make sure that we remained alert until taps, the upperclassmen would visit us after supper for final indoctrination in the ways and customs of the military. From time-to-time they would also review our knowledge of aircraft recognition, code, and bulletin-board reading, as well as our General Orders.

Cleanliness was heavily stressed, as cadets, two and three deep in the latrines, vied for mirror space to shave in the post-reveille scramble to appear on the parade ground for morning roll-call. Morning temperatures were cold, and it was quite dark. As a result, it didn't take long for enterprising cadets to learn that the necessary greatcoats covered them to the extent that only shoes, socks and pants were necessary for this formation and one could then finish dressing "at leisure" upon returning to the barracks.

We also learned how to "GI" the barracks and were happy to learn that we were not assessed for the barracks cleaning equipment and supplies.

Academically we were introduced to Morse Code, Physics, maps, charts, Aerial Photograph Interpretation, and Naval Craft Identification. We also learned that there was a check-list for everything from bed-making to the conduct and duties of the latrine orderly. Anyone not taking these programs seriously or who did not function according to specification, would be assessed demerits which were worked off on your day off by walking tours in the square with field pack and rifle at the rate of one hour per demerit. Strangely enough, all of these advantages were provided at no cost to us; in fact, we even were paid at the rate of $75.00 per month plus $1.00 per day subsistence, and our uniforms and quarters were provided free-of-charge!

After the first two or three weeks in Preflight, if you had no demerits to walk off, you were given a pass to go to town. In this case the town was San Antonio. It was a rather nice town but the main attractions for the cadets were the "Aztek Theater" and the "Gunter Hotel." The theater was beautiful, built to look like the interior of an Aztek Temple, and they showed first-run movies. The Gunter Hotel was notable in that San Antonio women hosted a weekly reception for the cadets every Sunday afternoon. The womens' daughters were hostesses in their very proper attire, including white gloves; and they danced with the cadets and made sure they had plenty of punch and cookies. I suspect that lurking in the back of the mothers' minds was the hope that their daughters might find "suitable" husbands among these "exceptional" men.

After nine weeks of being prepared to become "Flying Officers," not just pilots, and designated "Class of 43-I," we said goodbye to this home away from home and headed for our Primary Training Base, Garner Field in Uvalde Texas. Those of us fortunate enough to be chosen for this assignment found a true oasis in the arid Texas landscape, about 80 miles west of San Antonio. It was a tiny dot on the endless map of Texas, but it was a delightful base. It was a civilian operation, a contract flight school, and was run as though the company was trying to entice students for training.

The quarters were like hotel suites for four cadets. They were clean, neat, and comfortable, with desks and reading lamps. The food was excellent and plentiful, and was eaten civilian style utilizing the whole seat of the chair if desired. There was lush grass everywhere that was not paved. All of our instructors, both flight and ground school, were civilians. There was even a beautiful, sparkling swimming pool available when you were not committed to other duties. An additional blessing was **"There were no upperclassmen!"** However, we soon came to believe that the Flying Officers who conducted our frequent check-rides were recruited from the worst of the upperclassman types and appeared to be frustrated sadists whose company we never found to be enjoyable.

Here, for the first time in the Army Air Corps, we saw airplanes. They looked beautiful to us with their two-tone blue and yellow color scheme. To me it was almost like being back in Allentown, Pennsylvania at Allen High School, with its Canary and Blue color motif. We were eager to "saddle up" on these colorful steeds even though their fabric-covered fuselages and plywood encased wings were not too reassuring to us. We were soon to find, however, that these PT-19's were sturdy little vehicles which could carry us through the worst Texas thermals that were ever created.

"A" Flight Aviation Cadets: W. A. Thorpurn (left), and Frank E. Speer were the only two Cadets, of six, to be advanced from Primary to Basic Training by instructor F.J. Bussell (standing).

Our new routine was Flight School in the morning and Flight Training in the afternoon, alternating with the reverse order the next day. It soon became apparent that morning flying was much more desirable than afternoon flying. The mornings presented a fairly stable air pattern while afternoons developed thermals that jerked the planes around with kidney-wrenching movements. In fact, the afternoons changed the appearance of many of the planes. One of the highlights of the noon meal was the tasty and colorful dessert which was served almost daily. It was a junket-type pudding, red one day, blue or yellow the next. Invariably, some of the afternoon flyers were unable to cope with the motions caused by the thermals and relieved their air-sick stomachs by "barfing" over the side of the open-cockpit planes. It seemed always that the ones who had yellow dessert were flying in planes with blue fuselages and those who had eaten blue or red pudding were flying in planes with yellow fuselages. In either event, the evidence was outstanding and the guilty cadet was not allowed to forget his misdeed as he was kidded unmercifully in addition to the ignominy of having to wash the evidence off his plane.

Unfortunately, this was not the only consequence of a cadet's airsickness. If the problem continued, after two or three more flights, the cadet was washed out of flight training and shipped out for reclassification along with others who were unable to pass the check-rides. During the time we spent in Primary, my instructor's class dropped from six to two of us, who were then advanced to Basic Training.

After nine or ten hours of flight training, those who had survived the rigors of airsickness and check-rides were faced with the inevitable do-it-yourself business of soloing. Everyone felt he could fly like a bird and that the solo could not come soon enough. Nevertheless, the event was approached with some trepidation, since making your first mistake could very well be your last, with no one to correct any error but you yourself. However, most passed with flying colors since the planes could almost land by themselves, and with their wide undercarriage were most unlikely to ground-loop. Having soloed, it was now fun to fly without a back-seater to remind you when you deviated a degree or two from course or a few feet from desired altitude.

After a week of pressured flying and heavy ground school assignments, weekend passes were a pleasant interlude. They were made even more pleasant since my wife, Marge, had arrived from Pennsylvania. It must have taken a lot of courage to travel alone from Pennsylvania to Texas in a Greyhound bus but she did it. Unbelievably, the cost of her round trip was less than $30.00 and she even got a refund when she decided to stay and not use the return ticket. She was fortunate in finding a room in a small boarding-house and almost immediately found a job to cover her expenses. With her in town and another cadet wife and her husband, we had many nice evenings in the local ice cream parlor, accompanied by cadets Reggie Stevenson, a very funny guy, and Joe Stager, another close friend. Reggie provided no end of entertainment with his impromptu sing-a-longs with the jukebox, his favorite being *Jukebox Saturday Night.*

Soon 156 of us who had survived the best the thermals and the gremlins could throw at us, passed our exams, and were transferred to Goodfellow Field in San Angelo, deep in the heart of Texas. Here we found a military base with all the military furnishings and all military officer instructors. It was definitely a different life. Reveille was blown on a bugle, not Glenn Miller's *Sunrise Serenade.* Here we were introduced to the BT-13, or as it was commonly known, "The Vultee Vibrator." It well deserved that name since at any advanced throttle setting it shook, rattled, and vibrated as if it were about to disintegrate. We now had more engine and a variable speed prop; and were introduced to cross-country flights (follow the iron beam), night flying, formation flying, and much, much more of the horrible Link Trainer exercises, and interminable bouts of dit-daw code practice. It is amusing to note that we spent endless stressful hours studying the full alphabet in Morse Code only to discover we would only use the "A" and "N" letters in code in the beam orientation of instrument flying. We never had any other occasion to use Morse Code in our flying careers.

It was not the fun time that we had in Uvalde, and after our nine week assignment, we were glad to move on to our next stop at Moore Field in Mission, Texas. This was about as far south as you could go and still be in the United States. With a strong tail wind, you could almost spit to the Rio Grande. Crossing that river on pass led some of the cadets to new types of adventures.

Now we found a real airplane, well-powered, with a variable speed prop, and retractable landing gear. I was an absolute dream to fly; a real pilot's plane; the AT-6. Here it began to look like we meant business. We were introduced to gunnery, first with a "BB" Link Trainer which shot BBs as you "flew" an earth-bound Link, firing at small plane targets moving around on a curving track, and then with a 30-caliber machine gun mounted on an AT-6, firing at a towed target. All I can say is the pilot of the tow target plane must have had a death wish to accept that job. Fortunately, we all survived the last firing course which found us diving and firing on ground targets.

The next episode found us flying in exciting, under-powered, nose-heavy, war-weary P-40s. In spite of their deficiencies, this was beyond a doubt the most excitement we'd had in months. The P-40 was maneuverable and fun to fly and made us feel like real "hot shots." We shared these 40's with Chinese airmen, most of whom could speak only limited English. We soon learned that when we heard over the radio, "Clear Lunlay, Chinee boy come landling," he meant it and we got as far away as possible. The fact that they meant it was clear to see since frequently they overshot and the brush beyond the end of the runway was cleared to P-40 wing level for several hundred feet by these determined airmen.

It is interesting to note our cadet attitude towards our Director of Training, Col. Henry Spicer, a combat veteran who was rumored to be in excess of forty years old. He could "wring-out" a P-40 with the best of them, but we cadets couldn't understand how such an *old* man could stand up to the rigors of flying a real combat plane.

Finally, after all nine months of this rigorous training, the class of 43-I graduated. It was a different world; we almost went broke buying our initial set of "Pinks and Greens" with the meager uniform allowance the Government gave us. But it sure was great to put on the spanking new "Wings" and the Lieutenant Bars we had so laboriously earned. It was even a pleasure to give a dollar to the first enlisted man who saluted us, an old Army custom.

Our final destination was Dale Mabry Field near Tallahassee, Florida, where we trained in the greatest prop fighter ever produced, the P-51 Mustang. What a plane it was, and we immediately fell in love with it. It was an airborne sports-car with power to spare, and an absolute delight to fly, in spite of the fact that I was very cramped in the model B's cockpit. Here I lost the first of my friends to die in the training program. He augured in to the swamp on a ground-strafing mission and drowned. I also had the unusual experience of being shot down over Florida by a careless pilot firing hot rounds left in the guns by an equally careless armament man. Fortunately, only the plane suffered damage although I suffered minor damage to my pride. Shortly thereafter, we headed for the Port of Embarkation and new adventures on another continent.

Chapter I

THE LUST FOR ACCEPTANCE

A well-worn "78" turns out the familiar strains of Glenn Miller's *Sunrise Serenade*. The melody seems compressed into the corner of the Ready-Room by the overpowering sounds of the other activities of the squadron pilots, nervously killing moments while awaiting the departure time of the day's mission.

The Flight Surgeon, probably the only completely calm man in the room, is busily engaged in playing Cribbage with one of the new pilots, whose tension is even more apparent when contrasted with the serenity of his inscrutable opponent. Although apparently completely absorbed in the game, Dr., now Captain, Cecil Blackburn, is closely observing his opponent for the telltale symptoms of combat fatigue. If sufficient symptoms were apparent, he would be pulled off combat operations and given a short leave to calm his nerves and bring his thoughts and reactions back into proper perspective. A jumpy pilot can be a dangerous man in a tight situation where instant, logical decisions mean the difference between life and death to others as well as to himself.

Four men, half-heartedly, alternate at nudging a cue ball in an attempt to appear interested in a game of pool, their eyes shaded by the visors of their "Forty Mission Crush" uniform hats, the symbol of their glamorous but very dangerous occupation.

A small group listens while a Midwestern farm boy, recently

turned hot-shot pilot, tells of the marvelous exploits of his hopped-up Chevy back in Bloomington, Indiana. Each one of the group is eager to jump into the conversation to top his story with an exaggerated exploit of his own.

On the other side of the room, another knot of pilots talk shop about the last mission over "Flak Alley" and how the Germans have stiffened their defense by moving more fighters into the area.

The final notes of *Sunrise Serenade* are followed by the clicking of the worn mechanism of the rapidly-aging record player as Bing Crosby's *Mandy is Two* falls into place and the "Groaner" competes in the cacophony of sounds. The tension grows perceptibly as each minute passes. Each of the pilots is repeating his own conscious or subconscious ritual, a ritual performed almost exactly the same way, time after time, as a prelude to each mission. Each individual ritual is designed, and gradually refined, in an effort to appear unconcerned about the uncertainties ahead. It is an effort to preclude the intrusion of anyone else into the inner mind where an individual might not be completely convinced of his own personal invincibility. Each tries hard to believe and even harder to project his feelings of invincibility to his associates by appearing nonchalant and unconcerned; some are quite convincing, others are obviously tentative in their conviction.

Captain Blackburn calmly drones, "Fit-een two, fit-een four, and two is six," and quickly shuffles the deck as the pilot records the score with a makeshift peg in the worn Cribbage board. With a flare almost too professional, the Captain rapidly deals the cards and, picking up his hand, casually fans them with one hand, like a well-practiced magician. The surgeon's hands are versatile and the long fingers flexible and obviously trained for the exacting work of surgery. He is one of the very few who can manipulate three one-shilling coins equally well with either hand. He can raise either end coin and turn it over to restack it neatly between the other two, or raise the center coin, turn it over and restack it back between the other two in its original slot. Over and over, this pastime is practiced daily by almost everyone on the base with any semblance of manual dexterity, who might happen to have three one-shilling coins in his pocket. Many try, but few, even with the dominant hand, can match the dexterity of the Flight Surgeon, who appears to be ambidextrous.

At the command, "Atten-hut," all activities immediately cease and silence falls over the room as the pilots stand at attention. Colonel Blakeslee strides briskly into the room and barks "At Ease." The command comes easily, but there is no question that he is in total charge and that no nonsense will be tolerated. There is a flurry of activity as the pilots find seats and then the curtain covering the huge map on the wall at the front of the room is drawn. A subdued murmuring ensues at the sight of the many long colored lines stretching far into the heartland of Germany.

The mission for *today* is a long one. The lines on the map stretch across the continent to Saarbrucken in the heart of the Saar valley. The different colored lines, zigzagging across the map, indicate a big show and one most likely to encourage heavy enemy resistance. The schedule is complex, as P-47s escort the bombers to a rendezvous with a P-51 Group that then escorts them to the target where they are to be relieved by our Group. We are to take over escort through the target area and cover them as they regroup to head home. We, in turn, are to be relieved by 51s who will escort them on their way back to England. The weather briefing indicates good conditions with minimal cloud cover over the target. The hunting should be good and, although no one will articulate the thought, each one knows in his heart that there will most likely be empty seats in the mess hall tonight. Although each pilot refuses to consider in his own mind that he might be one of those who do not return, the odds inexorably close in on him each time he is posted to fly a mission. There have been many names deleted from the ready-roster, and there will be many more, "C'est la Guerre."

Of those who do not immediately return, some will be fortunate and reach the Channel, ditch or "hit the chute" and be picked up by one of the plucky little rescue vessels constantly

Col. Donald Blakeslee briefs the 4th Fighter Group for a long combat mission, England to Russia Shuttle. (Manning)

Chesley Peterson briefs 334 Fighter Squadron on the day's mission.

roaming the Channel, under the very noses of the German shore batteries and coastal defense boats. Some may reach "Land's End" and belly-in their crippled kites to join the ignominious graveyard of many other planes that have reached their final resting place before them. Some will be bulldozed off the landing area and others will be unceremoniously stripped of all usable parts and left to lie like nameless cadavers in a medical school class.

Some pilots may be less fortunate and have their flying careers prematurely ended, sitting out the remainder of the hostilities as guests of the Luftwaffe, a future too unpleasant to even consider for those so accustomed to the freedom of the skies. For others, the always-present possibility exists, that life on Earth could be ended before the day is over. In either of these cases, the name will be deleted from the roster, the man's effects sent home, and the business of the Group will go on. There is no time and no good to come of dwelling on these inevitable misfortunes. The Chaplain and the Commanding Officer will take care of the final details, including the letter to the next-of-kin, one of their most unpleasant duties.

The turnover of pilots in this Group is high. This probably accounts for the fact that there are few long-term buddies among them. It also could be the reason why replacement pilots are not "socially accepted" immediately. Each pilot seems to, more or less, insulate himself from the pain of losing a close friend. Each, in effect, becomes a loner in the midst of his team. He may be congenial at the bar, but he sleeps with only his intimate thoughts as his true companions.

Out on the flight line, the crew chiefs are nervously going over the checklists again and again while the crews fiddle with valves, gauges, and miscellaneous hardware. They check over and over again, to make sure no detail has been overlooked in the preparation of their magnificent "Merlin"-powered flying machines. Each of these men is as proud of his plane as is a fine musician tuning his Stradivarius for the ultimate concert. The concert, however, could end in a crescendo of glory or the infamy of defeat; or even the untimely death of their pilot, at the moment of truth. No one wants to carry the awesome burden of failure in his duty to his team, a real and constant fear to these men whose "Esprit de Corps" will not allow them to consider failure. Gas tanks are checked and rechecked, radios tuned and adjusted and retuned, gun mechanisms tested and retested; no detail is overlooked. There can be no aborts today.

As departure time approaches, pilots nervously glance at the back of their hands, almost as often as they breathe, where the statistics of the mission were carefully recorded during the briefing. There it is handy for reference but easy to obliterate, in case capture is imminent.

For hours the sky has been full of the droning sounds of the overloaded bombers, laboriously grasping for another inch of altitude. Relentlessly, they have been climbing into the ever thinning, ever colder, ever more hostile atmosphere, forming into the tight defensive formations which give them the scathing defensive firepower of an aerial battleship. They started their mission while most of the fighter pilots were fitfully sleeping, blissfully unaware of the magnitude of the pending mission.

The tension mounts steadily. The pool table is forgotten. The "78's" huddle at the bottom of the turntable, the mechanism, unheard, having ground to a halt. In the corner, the Flight Surgeon makes an entry in his little book as his uninterested opponent sits numbly contemplating the impending announcement of the names of today's participants. I hear my name included as one of them.

Once the names are announced, there are a couple of last reminders, by S-2, (Intelligence) preceding the distribution of the escape kits, in their little olive drab vests. They are worn under the pilots' flight jackets, for that ever possible, "just in case." These vests are remarkable repositories of the minimal essentials necessary for a pilot to sustain life in the event he is downed in a situation where he can evade capture for an extended period of time. Fishhooks, compasses, first aid supplies, Halizone tablets, and money are compactly placed in different pockets along with a "Forty-five," complete with bird shot as well as ball ammunition.

A few words are offered by the Chaplain, for those who are interested, and there are few who are not. We then pile out the door and into the waiting trucks. The resourceful overloaded vehicles speed off into the gathering dawn, peeling off separately into waiting revetment areas to deliver their cargo of shivering pilots to their eager steeds. Dispersed around the field, huddling close to their ever-watchful revetments, stand the mighty Mustangs. Their bright-red noses glisten with a coating of early morning dew. Their sleek gray-green fuselages, looking drab in the half-light, give no indication of the tremendous drive and responsiveness of the 1650 horsepower engines hidden within their cowls. The engines, a designer's dream, Packard-built Rolls-Royces, were the first ever to develop over a horsepower per pound of engine weight. They stand ready to surge to life at the touch of the starter. The huge four-bladed props wait impatiently for the moment they are called upon to turn the powerful engine's output into useful thrust.

This beautiful, angular machine is a highly maneuverable flying gun platform, whose six fifty-caliber machine guns carry the capability to knock a railroad engine off its tracks, or chew an enemy plane to bits. Its range, aided by two ingeniously adapted 108 gallon wing tanks, is such that no place in Germany can provide a sanctuary from its deadly threat. It is a match for anything the Germans can mount against it, and we pilots love it like no other plane that exists.

One by one, the pilots and their gear are dropped off in front of their planes. Finally, my truck jolts to a stop in front of a plane bearing the insignia of a fat, bomb-carrying insect, sighting through a pair of flying goggles and firing two blunderbusses held in its six feet. The name "Turnip Termite" stretches out behind its diving body. I spring to the ground and throw a friendly salute to the waiting crew. Following a complete visual check of the plane and its components, I clamber onto the wing, closely followed by Crew Chief, Bill Brong.

Bill is as fine a crew chief as anyone could want, responsive to every need and dedicated to having "his" plane available for more hours of duty than any other in the Group. "Mae-West" in place, I carefully strap on my dinghy and parachute and struggle into the cramped quarters of the instrument-laden cockpit. Here I will spend the next few hours uncomfortable, but happy to be flying this world-class machine. By slouching slightly, my head clears the canopy and my shoulders barely touch its sides. It would be claustrophobic were it not for the surrounding expanse of glass. I remember the warning I was given when I entered Aviation Cadet training, "You will never be a fighter pilot, you are too big!" However, having graduated at the top of my class and having been 3rd highest scorer in aerial gunnery training, I somehow was assigned to fighters. Possibly the need for fighter pilots was greater than the desire to make me comfortable.

Bill helps me to adjust the double shoulder harness and secure it to the seat-belt with its breakaway latch which can be instantly released by a touch, freeing the pilot to escape in the event of an emergency.

The cockpit routine is completed; the controls, oxygen and radio are checked. The prop pitch control is rammed forward to the stop, the mixture control set to full rich for maximum power, and the throttle is cracked. The crew chief responds to my cry, "clear," and the starter is engaged. Slowly, the prop turns, gathering speed, the engine coughs twice and suddenly roars to life as if released from some desultory prison. The OK sign is passed to me from the crew chief, the battery cart umbilical cord is pulled, followed by the chocks, and the magnificent kite with its throbbing engine slowly pulls away from the revetment.

There is a slight wait for the appropriate place in line of the many aircraft weaving their way to the take-off position, and then it's follow the leader to the end of the runway. The weaving right and left, is to allow the pilots to see ahead, since the long Merlin engine blocks the view directly forward. When my plane is next in line to take-off, I "run-up" the engine to check the mags for proper operation, give the gauges one final check, and then in

Lt. Frank Speer signs flight record upon return from a mission. Crew Chief Bill Brong (center) and lineman anxiously await the results.

The "Turnip Termite" assigned to Lt. Speer displays its fierce visage.

prearranged sequence, I find myself in position with my element leader, ready for take-off. The signal is given for take-off, and we ram everything forward for maximum power. The responsive engines take us roaring down the runway as inertia presses us against the seat back. A short run and seemingly effortlessly, our graceful fighters become airborne and we raise the wheels to slowly come to nest in the accommodating wing-roots. Gently, we change the prop pitch and lean the mixture-control, and the planes respond by rapidly picking up speed as we begin a wide, graceful, climbing turn. The turn continues, ever upward, allowing following planes to turn in a shorter arc and eventually catch up to the lead planes, until all have joined together. They then assemble into their assigned slots in the Squadron combat formation. Elements of two join to become Flights of four; Flights of four join to become Squadrons; and finally, the three Squadrons join to become the Group. The "Fourth Fighter Group," destined to make history, is on its way, and everyone is honed to a fine edge for today's bout with the Nazis' best.

As the last planes to take-off join the formation, the course is set for the scheduled rendezvous with the bombers. Strict radio silence is maintained, and the sense of being alone grows steadily. As the formation continues its steady climb, the sky becomes lighter and lighter until abruptly, our planes burst out of the haze into the full glare of the morning sun. Suddenly there is the thrill and exhilaration of breaking the bonds of earth, a feeling felt only by those who fly; an excitement that cannot be shared through even the most descriptive of words.

The thrill is short-lived as the mundane demands of flying and staying alive must be met. As the steady climb continues, and the air becomes less dense, the mixture controls are adjusted for the most efficient air/gas ratio in order to conserve fuel for the long mission ahead. The loose formation continues ever upward, and the pilots check their oxygen equipment for proper function. To fail in this, invites a gradual numbing of the senses and euphoria followed by complete loss of rational thought and eventual blackout as "anoxia," the result of the lessening of air pressure at high altitudes, diminishes the lungs' ability to absorb oxygen. The blood is consequently no longer able to supply adequately the demands of the oxygen-starved brain, which then ceases to function normally and finally protests by blacking out. There is no warning to the pilot that this is about to happen, and he continues on, blissfully unaware that his actions are less and less rational, and that he will soon become unconscious.

Now crossing the Channel in the warmth of the morning sun, thoughts may stray to home, wives, and families. Possibly, even a moment is allowed for fantasy. A moment to dream of the possibility of being a hero of the day by single-handedly fighting overwhelming numbers of enemy planes and emerging victorious. More soberly, a fantasy or wish most likely would be for the opportunity to engage, at least once, in man-to-man aerial combat, and to be victorious beyond all shadow of doubt. This would be most reassuring to a pilot who might not otherwise be sure that he has the essential mental qualifications to stand up to the life and death situations he most assuredly will encounter. Some might prefer to remain on the sideline and play it safe. What will he do? Until the first victory, there is always a question. Here in this Group I feel so insignificant, amid the ones who have survived months or even years of combat against the Germans. They have all faced the enemy and proven to themselves and their peers that they have the right stuff. Now, to me, the burden of proof rests on me, no one else. I hunger for the opportunity to prove, if only to myself, that I am truly a part of this outstanding organization. There are more aces in this Group than have ever been assembled in any other Allied Group in history. I know that I have had better training, and better equipment than many of them have had, and better indoctrination, but do I really have what's necessary to belong? One day soon I will find out. I want to be accepted by the members of this elite Group, without the least bit of doubt!

Flying in the shadow of these men who have flown with the RAF or the RCAF in the Battle of Britain, places an awesome responsibility on the shoulders of a new replacement pilot, freshly graduated from the Army Air Corps flight school. These pilots had the vision to realize that this war was not just the "Europeans' war" and, in spite of the dire consequences for doing so, they had the guts to leave the U.S. In effect, they jeopardized their lives as well as their citizenship to do what they felt was right. To follow in their footsteps is an honor I cannot take lightly. Even though I have had the best training in the world, I hope impatiently for the opportunity to prove that these efforts have not been in vain.

To put everything in perspective, there are also a very few who I do not want to emulate, who have more missions, possibly more sense, and certainly less need for acceptance. They think more of putting in their required number of missions necessary to be rotated back to the States to finish out the war in the relative safety of such occupations as flight instructor or ferry pilot, amid the adulation of those who have yet to earn their "Stripes."

Of special note are those who can be considered "hard corps," such as Captain Sobanski, our Squadron Leader. He was a Pole, whose experiences fighting the Hun as an infantryman, and later as a prisoner, motivates him to a high level of hatred. He thinks only of killing as many Germans as possible. This consuming force drives him to be the most meticulous taskmaster a pilot could ever have as a squadron commander. He wants no safety of rotation, he wants only to fight, for as long as there is an enemy left to fight.

Chapter II

THE SQUADRON COMMANDER

The Captain was born Winslow Mickael Sobanski, in New York City on 29 July 1919, while his mother was visiting her sister on a vacation from her home in Poland. While there, she also visited her close friends, Harry Bruno, and his wife Nydia. Harry had been a WWI, RCAF pilot and was a well-known public relations consultant. Actually, he was responsible for the meeting of Mike's father and mother. Mike's father was an American-born Pole, residing in New York. In 1915, Baron and Baroness Jerczy de Sosnowski visited Bruno on a Russian military mission. They were accompanied by their daughter, Nydia, and her companion, Edja. In the course of events, Bruno married Nydia, and Mike's father married Edja. This close relationship resulted in Mike looking upon Harry Bruno as his "uncle."

Shortly after Mike was born, the family returned to Poland where Mike received his education. He was an economics student in a prestigious business college SGH (Szola Glowna Handlowa) when the Nazis invaded Poland. He and a few other students tried to join the Polish Air Force. The Polish Air Force was no match for the modern fighter planes of the Nazis and was soon defeated. Mike and his friends volunteered for the infantry and headed towards the front on a troop train. The train was bombed and Mike was pinned in the wreckage and suffered three broken ribs. His friends dug him out and got him on a train for transport to a hospital.

Hardly able to breathe, due to his broken ribs, with no food, Mike spent five tortuous days in a filthy boxcar on the way to an unknown destination. He arrived at an old monastery which was being used as a hospital, and waited two more days before they could treat him. Meanwhile, he watched as more serious cases were carried in for treatment. He endured the presence of ether, blood, sweat, amputations, dirt, and suffering. They finally put a cast on him but by then the Germans were closing in. Mike got out of bed, cast and all, and climbed aboard a Red Cross train headed east. The effort was in vain. The Germans arrived and captured the fleeing group. They were then moved by lorry to a hospital in an old Russian fort surrounded by a moat.

Mike, believed by the Germans to be immobile, was left unguarded. He again left the hospital, waded through the moat and hitch-hiked and walked 200 miles to Warsaw. There he found his home in ruins and the city under Nazi control. He happened to encounter his father who, as an infantry colonel had been defeated and was totally depressed. His father stayed in Warsaw but Mike had more urgent things on his mind.

As an American citizen, Mike was not harassed as were the Poles and the Jews. He soon applied for permission to leave and eventually it was granted. By a devious route, he then made his way to Venice, arriving with ten cents in his pocket, but happily out of Germany. He got out of Italy as a seaman aboard the American ship, the *Winston Salem*. He arrived in Baltimore and made his way to New York. He met with Harry Bruno who arranged for him to join the RCAF. He had many troubles in learning to fly because of his inability to speak or understand English, which he studied in his spare time. Mike even "washed out" of the training program because of this deficiency. Mike stated his frustration, "George Gilbert, son of a bitch, dirty bastard, washed me out in Goderich. Four bloody months wasted in a manning pool, sitting on my ass and doing nothing." Finally, through Bruno's intervention, he was readmitted to flight training, and he finally earned his wings in October 1941.

In his diary, dated 13th November 1941 he wrote; "Left Halifax, Nova Scotia aboard *Louis Pasteur* on 3rd November 1941. No excitement on the way over, except for Black Jack games, and one bad 100 mph wind storm, which nearly turned the boat over. A large supply of Scotch kept us in good spirits and helped to avoid sea-sickness. After ten days of zigzagging all over the Atlantic, we finally arrived at Greenock, Scotland. From there we went on. We traveled by night. Every couple of hours some RAF stewards would wake us up with a shout: *"Wakee, Wakee!"* and bring in enormous cups of tea. At first we thought the *"Wakee, Wakee"* stuff was just a gag. Soon, however, we were to discover that this together with *"bags"* of other English expressions was *"actually"* on the level. George Cadmus, one of my comrades, made another discovery, that every 50 miles or so, people have a different accent, and use a different slang. It amused George a great deal, as he exclaimed: 'Can you beat that! People, who live 50 miles apart, and in the same country, can hardly understand each other."

By the end of November, Mike was posted to Montrose, Scotland accompanied by Bob Williams (nicknamed Digger, because of his ability to always find himself in trouble), Pete Carter, Harper and Joe. Mike, from Poland and Pete Carter–South Africa, went to Montrose while their other friends of their *International Four* club from his RCAF days (George Cadmus–Argentina, and Jack Berry–USA) were shipped off to Coningsby, Lincolnshire to train in bombers. In Montrose, Mike was delighted to find that this was a fighter-pilot school where they were to train in Miles Masters and Hurricanes.

Mike and Pete were granted a leave and went to London where they stayed with Pete's uncle who lived there. Upon their arrival in London, they went to Selfridges American Restaurant for lunch. As they entered, Mike heard an excited voice "Wacek," and was amazed to see Wanda Lubowa, a good friend of his mother's, whom he had known for years. They had a warm reunion, talking about old times and they proceeded to get drunk together.

Later, Mike went to the American Eagle Club since he had learned that if he registered with them, he could buy cigarettes tax-free, a decided saving. While there he reinforced his desire to become a member of the Eagle Squadron when he became eligible, because he felt the Americans were well-organized and cared for their citizens. He believed a person had to be a real loser not to appreciate American citizenship. Mike felt that Europeans didn't understand Americans but at the Eagle Club, he felt a kinship with the Americans. The Eagle Club also had a radio broadcast every Thursday where American boys could say a few words to their families. Mike declined to speak to his parents, however, because they were in Warsaw and he was afraid the Germans might persecute them for having a son who was an active enemy.

Mike liked London and visited whenever he could. He always looked for and seemed to find Polish airmen, with whom he felt a strong bond. He was American by birth, and he was American by desire and choice, but he also felt he was a Polish patriot as well and his ties to Poland were strong and enduring. He grew up in Poland, his family was in Poland, his friends were in Poland, and last but not least by any thought, Marishia, his love, the woman he longed to marry, was in Poland.

In London, he soon learned that to be admitted to the numerous clubs, you needed an invitation or a membership. It also was necessary to be a member in order to buy liquor or to meet "decent" women. Mike being a normal young man was fond of both. It disturbed him greatly that officers had the upper hand in acquiring either. Being a Sergeant Pilot, he resented the disparity of treatment both in the social and the military life. He felt he was in the lowest level of the social order. He particularly hated the fact that many rear-echelon officers who never would see combat, ranked higher in regard than he, he who had been and was preparing again to engage in activities designed to kill the detested Germans. He hated the Germans with a fierce passion

Top-(left) Sgt Mike Sobanski Models RAF flight gear while (right) he displays his new Lieutenant's uniform upon joining the US Army Air Corps. Note the absence of his RAF wings.(Kirkup) Bottom-Mike's first assigned Spitfire in Army Air Corps, 336 Fighter Squadron, 4th Fighter Group (Kirkup)

Top-Eagle Squadron pilots have a "bull" session in front of a Spitfire prior to their transfer to the US Army Air Corps. Bottom-4ᵀᴴ Fighter Group pilots in a "bull" session in front of a P-51B sporting "kill" crosses under the windshield. (Konsler)

This Royal Canadian Air Force Insignia and the following black background drawings were freehand drawings in white ink on black photo album paper. They were meticulously crafted by Mike Sobanski while in the RCAF and the RAF.

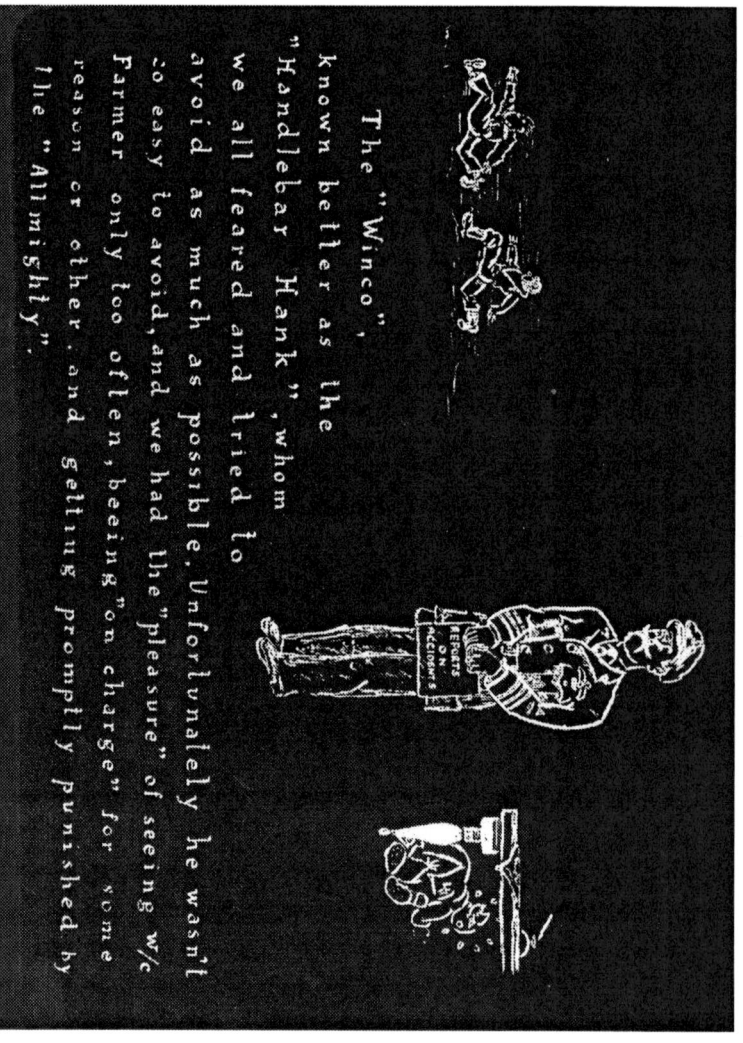

The "Winco", known better as the "Handlebar Hank", whom we all feared and tried to avoid as much as possible. Unfortunately he wasn't too easy to avoid, and we had the "pleasure" of seeing w/c Farmer only too often, beeing "on charge" for some reason or other, and getting promptly punished by the "Allmighty".

Interviews with the Wing Commander were never solicited.

The Instructor, Pilot Officer "Prune," had a dog with an interesting ancestry, by "Intruder out of Bandit"

Lessons were not always of a positive nature, but were great fun.

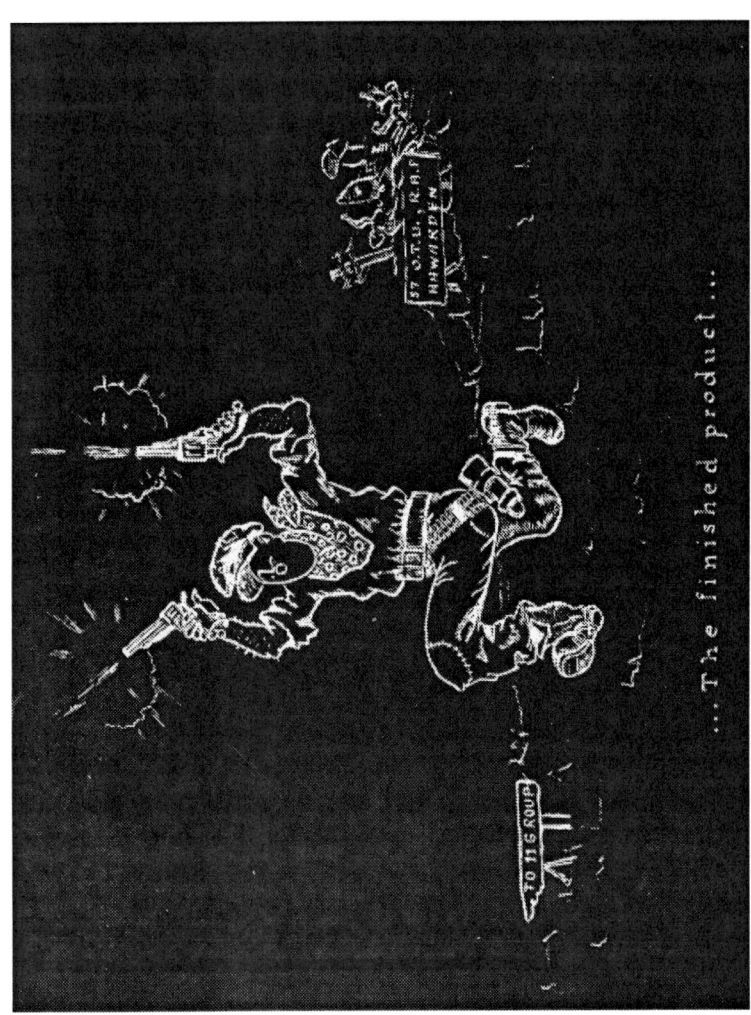

Graduation from OTU (Overseas Training Unit) created a new breed of cowboy.

...This is what happened one day... An A.T.A. (Air Transport Auxiliary) pilot was taxying over rough ground, with a "erk" (groundcrew man) sitting on the tail to hold it down. The A.C.P. (Aerodrome Control Pilot) gave him a green light, so he turned on the runaway and took off. The erk did not have time to jump off, or maybe thought the pilot would stop, after turning into wind. Anyway the Hurricane became airborne, with the erk clinging desperately to its tail. It would be hard to describe the panic on the drome: the ACP shooting red flares, op's & some pilots calling on the R/T etc. Finally the pilot noticed the "Hurri" was "a bit" tail-heavy and landed. The erk had a "free" ride of 2 circuits over Chester, stepped off, smiled & fainted. (The RAF gave him "24 hrs. off"... and a medical check...!)

An "erk" gets an unexpected ride.

for what they had done to his country as well as to himself, and for what they were doing to the rest of Europe. Mike expressed his frustration, " I am very pissed when I am thinking about this."

When his furlough was over, Mike went to his new post, an RAF base in Montrose, Scotland. When he arrived, one of his first stops was at the post theater where they were showing an anti-Nazi film *Freedom Station*. It set his blood to boiling as he saw the black-uniformed Gestapo in action. It made him think of Poland when his friends and their families were arrested and taken away. He was infuriated by these "bastards" and felt he couldn't wait to get a crack at them. That night he dreamed of killing the damn black-uniformed bastards. To make matters worse, the next morning he was to show up for the usual "short-arm inspection" and no doctors arrived. It seemed that everything about this station aggravated him.

His anger extended to the inferior treatment of non-coms at the Airbase. In December, it was bitter cold and heat for their rooms was unavailable. His room had a fireplace but there was no coal. One night when it was so cold they could not sleep, at 4 am, Harper stole some coal from the basement and Mike scrounged some old boards from the attic and they started a fire in the fireplace. Soon the word spread, and their room was filled with friends who came in to get warm. The caretaker came in to protest the theft of his coal, but they soon banished him with the advice that they had rights too, even though they were not commissioned officers.

Mike felt that the chance of being commissioned was practically nil. He knew of a Sergeant who had been awarded the highest British award, the VC, (Victoria Cross) and after two more years, was still a Sergeant. He felt that his education level and that of his friends was such as to warrant them becoming officers. George had graduated from a university, Harper had been studying medicine, Williams would have been a 2nd Lt., had it not been for a misadventure with a woman, and Mike himself had been studying at SGH.

Mike became very disappointed with this Montrose base. It was an RAF base, and unlike his previous RCAF base in Canada, he felt it was very disorganized. Mike summed it up, "The RAF is a piss-poor organization, no wonder they lost their asses in the fight at Dunkirk."

The following evening, Mike and Pete went to London again and ran into Digger and Harper. They all decided to have a few drinks and to go dancing. Mike asked a very handsome blonde to dance. They talked awhile and discovered that they had many mutual likes and dislikes and soon they were dancing cheek-to-cheek. In no time Wynile and Mike were closer and closer. When the dance was over, he walked her home, or rather to a street corner near her home, which was as close as she wanted him to go. Mike found the blackout conditions to be advantageous when interested in making love. He asked for a kiss, she complied willingly. " She was nice, she was married, she had soft skin, lips, tender and small, and a tiny well-built body. She was closer and closer with every kiss. She kept repeating 'I must go home' but she couldn't leave." Mike reminisced later as he found his way home, "We Polish and American guys have a reputation for being big womanizers and perfect lovers, I hope I didn't destroy this image."

As time went on, Mike met many Polish officers. They were amazed to see him dressed in a Canadian uniform with British wings, and a USA on his shoulder, and speaking perfect Polish. They often tried to talk him into changing into a Polish uniform. Mike's reply was always, "I am an American, I feel like an American, and I am happy to live in the States." He thought to himself, " I wouldn't give it up. The States are the greatest country in the World and one can be proud to belong to it. I am attracted to the American life-style. I am going to stay in the RCAF, and, for the moment, not interested in changing to the Eagle Squadron." He adopted a wait-and-see attitude, feeling strongly that he wanted to do something "really big" without the benefit of being with people strictly of his own "society."

Eventually, things became more organized and they settled

down to flying. The quarters were decent, with a fireplace which unfortunately gave off very little heat. He received his equipment in preparation for flying Hurricanes after completing his indoctrination in Miles Masters.

Mike lamented his inability to send letters to Marishia. He thought longingly of her, for he knew she had no idea where he was or what he was doing. He and his buddies listened constantly to the radio in their spare time and kept up with all the war news. They listened to Churchill and Roosevelt whenever they spoke. They were eager to get into the action of combat.

Mike was afraid that his seemingly endless training would keep him from combat before the end of the war. He and his friends were jubilant when the attack at Pearl Harbor thrust the USA into the war. They felt this would speed the end of their training and their entry into combat.

Soon they were flying in the Master. Weather often delayed their training causing Mike to exclaim in utter frustration, "This is the worst Goddamn climate I've ever seen in my life." Mike was not impressed with the Master's stiffer, clumsy on the controls characteristics and its plywood wings. He longed for the day he would begin flying the Hurricane. Nevertheless, his training continued with steep turns, forced landing practice and use of flaps. Then there was formation flying and dogfighting. Initially, he had a few instances where he forgot to put down his wheels or put down the wrong degree of flaps upon landing. However, he always remembered at the last instant and averted an embarrassing prang.

On the 19th of December, the big day arrived-his first flight in a Hurricane! He was scared at first, no instructor to help with this one, and to make matters worse, Sgt. Franklin, from the RAF, nosed over in a Hurricane during the morning. Mike signed the appropriate papers regarding knowledge of the Hurricane's engine and flight limitations and off he went. He charged down the runway, took off and was "climbing like hell," forgetting to change the prop pitch and was at 2,000 feet before he got everything in order. Later, when attempting to land he didn't like his approach so he pulled up the wheels and went around again. This time he landed but was heading straight for a Hurricane parked at the end of the field. He had a choice; slam on the brakes and nose over, or risk a ground loop by trying to avoid the parked plane. He chose the latter, barely missing the plane, but he was able to recover and avoid an accident.

He had visions of the crash truck screaming towards him and of being washed out, but no one seemed to have noticed so he taxied back and took off again, content to think, "That's an idiotic place to park an airplane, they couldn't choose worse!" Again he came in for a landing and surprised himself with a nice landing. "Just closed the throttle and brushed her in nice and smooth." He had been exuberant with his ability to make steep turns, never losing a foot of altitude, and felt this had to be the best plane in the war! Thus convinced he took her up for aerobatics; rolls, steep turns, stalls, and dives. On the way back to the base, he opened the hood and gloried in the feel of the speed of his newest love. His euphoria soon changed, for upon landing he found that Franklin had crashed. There was his plane, tail up and the propeller in the ground.

That night he lamented the fact that he could not write to Marishia. He felt so close to her as he thought "flying a Hurricane with its speed, I could be in Warsaw in three hours." He wrote in his diary, "To be with you for a moment, I would give everything. I am missing you so much. Goodnight Marriane, be in my dreams, goodnight, sweetheart." He always ended his letter writing sessions by saying "goodnight, Mary," or "goodnight, Marishia," or "goodnight" to any one of the pet names he had for his beloved Marishia.

Soon it was Christmas and after a night of fun, as might be expected, on Christmas Day, the men all slept in till afternoon. They then went for a feast the likes of which they hadn't seen since Canada, complete with turkey, the usual side dishes, and ending with real coffee. After the meal, they left for town, and found themselves at "Angus Dance." There were quite a few Polish servicemen there and they sang Polish Christmas songs.

There were also several women with whom they were flirting. About 12 pm, everyone started greeting one another and the guys were kissing all the girls. By this time they were all fairly drunk.

Mike cozied up to Margaret. She was very pretty, but didn't even know how to kiss. He walked her home after the party and as usual asked for a kiss. "She had soft young lips, still very girlish and she was so innocent. I kissed her and I felt like I got drunk more from this kiss than I did from all the alcohol." Mike thought "Such a young innocent creature; I can't keep her longer even though she is willing, I don't want her to fall in love with me. Then what would I do? I'm not going to marry her; I don't want to be dishonest with her. I cannot give her my love because Marishia is in my blood and every nerve is calling for her." Mike returned home thinking, " I miss Marishia, I miss my friends, I miss my father, I miss my family."

New Year's Day dawned and Mike, dejected, expressed himself, " I'm so unhappy, I'll be son of a bitch, 1942!!! It's horrible, two more years we'll have to suffer, two more years without letters from Marishia, or my father, about the war. I'm sick of this Montrose food; fish, pea soup, sausages, meat pie, stew and pudding with custard. We rarely get steak and they don't even have ketchup or pickles." Mike also fretted about what work he would be able to find after the war was ended. His morale was really at a low point. He began to feel he would never achieve his goal of being a combat fighter pilot "The Crazy Pole" and the first Polish-American pilot to be awarded the VC.

This mood was soon to change as shortly, Mike got word that they had hit the jackpot. They were moving to #61 O.T.U., Heston, a very good station about fifteen miles from London and they fly Spitfires. Mike's reaction was,"Yipee! Spitfires, Oh Boy! V for Victory, Hurray! 400 miles per hour, four machine guns and two cannons, I must write and tell Harry Bruno, he will be happy."

Rumors gave way to reality and Mike was sent to #57 O.T.U. at Hawarden, North Wales instead of Heston for his Spitfire training. Heavy snows and bitter cold, as Mike said, "like a whores heart" were the January norm while he awaited the opportunity for his first Spitfire flight. In the meantime, the class had lectures and Link training and they were introduced to the Hawarden Trainer. It was somewhat like a Link trainer but was fitted like a Spitfire cockpit.

On February 11, Mike's opportunity arrived. His first Spitfire flight. He took-off smoothly and exclaimed "she climbs like a son-of-a-bitch, I was at 3,000 feet before I closed the hood."

Mike's continued training was routine and by the end of May he was flying Convoy Patrol with the 416 Canadian Sq. out of Aberdeenshire, Scotland. He found this to be very boring but got some pleasure out of "beating up" convoys on occasion. In all the time he flew convoy patrol, he only ever saw two Nazi planes and only got off one burst at an out-of-range 109.

On September 22, 1942, he was discharged from the RAF, and posted to the 133 Eagle Squadron, along with Ray Fuchs and Jimmy Goodson as a 2ND Lt. On the 29th of September, they transferred to the 336 Squadron of the 4th Fighter Group, U.S. 8th Air Force.

It was there that I first met Mike. He was a handsome man with a slight scar on one side of his nose which gave him a slightly sinister look like a gentle Basil Rathbone. He was thin and athletic in build, and had the manner of one who could be found quite attractive by women. This of course did not affect the seriousness with which he regarded the discipline of flying. We soon learned that his leadership was demanding and strictly "no nonsense."

Chapter III

THE MISSION CONTINUES

As the mission drags on, I can't help but feel hopelessly alone in this huge formless sky with no sound but the steady drone of the powerful compassionless engine. Even this sound is so uniform, unchanging, and monotonous that it seems eventually to creep into silence. As if the Group Leader is aware of this hypnotic effect, suddenly, the silence is abruptly shattered by the command, "This is Cobweb Leader. Close it up and get those heads moving." Although it is unlikely, at this point in the mission, attack could come at any moment. Those pilots who return safely to base today, will be those who are constantly alert to this fact. They will continually search all areas of the sky, looking for minuscule dots or shadows in the far distance which could grow in size to become hostile aircraft, "Bandits," seeking to repel this invasion of their home territory. Those unrelenting "searchers" will be thankful that their parachute silk scarves protect their necks from the abrasive collars of their flight suits. The uninformed think that these scarves are fetishes of the bravado associated with fighter pilots, but actually they are very useful. They avoid chafing of the neck and help the pilot to keep warm, and all too frequently they are used as a temporary bandage or as a tourniquet in case of necessity.

The course is now set at ninety-three degrees, a setting calculated to counter the force of the cross-wind at cruising altitude to ensure the intercept with the bombers just south of the target. The planes sweep lazily back and forth across this course, increasing and decreasing altitude slightly, from time to time, but ever-maintaining combat speed. This mild evasive action is necessary to preclude the possibility of enemy anti-aircraft batteries being able to predict precisely where to aim in order to destroy their ever-moving targets: "*Us*!" It is most comforting to know of the lag in time between the firing of an ack-ack gun and moment at which the projectile arrives at its target or the point at which the target was computed to be at that moment, several miles above.

The evasive action is well-advised, as sporadic bursts of flak at three o'clock low indicate that the enemy is awake and waiting. The thick, black, ugly bursts, with their deadly jagged edges, also confirm the crossing of the unseen coastline in the murky morning atmosphere below. Needless to say, everyone takes a renewed interest in the evasive tactics as the ugly black, almost fascinating, bursts creep closer. It is of little comfort to know that the chances of a fighter being hit by flak at this altitude are remote, as long as the evasive action is continued with no pattern. Although the ground may be five miles below, some of those gunners are good, and with all the practice we give them, occasionally a gunner has been known to make a mistake or a very good guess and someone gets to make an unauthorized landing in Nazi-controlled territory. It can be by chute, by crash landing, or "KIA." Knowing the odds against being hit has never made me feel any more comfortable when the flak bursts around me. The Germans do their best to continue to make crossing the Coast a moment of anxiety, as crossing after crossing they doggedly present the same determined effort to make this crossing our last.

As suddenly as it started the flak ends, to the great relief of all concerned. From now on, until over the target, additional flak is unlikely. Now all efforts are devoted to constantly searching the remote edges of the sky for the first glimpse of the tiny dots which could indicate the presence of Bandits: the hunters hunting the hunters. Any fighter attack having the advantage of surprise has a greatly enhanced opportunity for success. To aid in the effort to be able to see the enemy before he sees us, the Group edges slowly upward searching for the area where the "contrails" begin to form. Contrails, the thin curtain of ice crystals formed by disturbing the stable, supersaturated air at high altitude, are a dead give-away. The production of contrails signals for miles the presence of aircraft and the direction of their travel. Once we have reached the level of contrail development, the Group drops down a couple hundred feet below this area to fly just below the critical level. At this altitude, any enemy seeking the advantage of attacking from a higher altitude must certainly expose himself by formation of this lacy trail, as he maneuvers to attack, and thereby lose the advantage of surprise.

Radio silence is abruptly broken as a voice declares, "Cobweb Leader, this is Cobweb Red Four, engine rough, aborting mission." A gruff response, "Roger, Cobweb Four," follows as one of the planes sweeps from the formation in a graceful arc and heads back towards the distant base at Debden. That pilot had a hard choice to make; the choice was between facing combat far over enemy territory, with an engine performing at less than one hundred percent, or facing an irate commanding officer should his engine prove fully operational. Any pilot who chooses to abort better have a well-defined operational problem when he lands, or he will have a rough encounter with his C.O when he returns from the day's mission. The crew chief will have to have an explanation why the equipment was malfunctioning or the pilot will have to explain why he aborted with fully operational equipment. An abort is by no means a comfortable operation. Unfortunately, an abort has been used on occasion to avoid a particularly dangerous mission, or to avoid the unpleasantness of a rough mission with a hangover from too much indulgence at the Officers' Club the night before. It is consequently a move of last resort, which is initiated only after full consideration of the possible unpleasant consequences. As the aborting plane heads back towards England, one of the alternates slides unceremoniously into the slot left open by the vacating plane.

Back at the base, the crews are ever aware of the possibility that any one of their planes could be forced to return prematurely. With this in mind, it is hard for them to relax. Their personal pride, of which there is abundance, is at stake each time their plane takes off. These men work hard and diligently at keeping their planes at peak performance. There is a strong rivalry among the crews, each crew wanting to have its plane available for more hours of combat each month than any of the other crews. To this end, it is not at all unusual for a crew to work all night to overcome some unusual problem with its plane in order that it can be operational for the next day's mission.

In order to cover their anxiety during a mission the crews engage intensely in activities such as volleyball, in which there is fierce inter-crew competition. Even though they may become seemingly totally absorbed in these competitive sports, each man unconsciously has an ear cocked for the first distant sound of a returning aircraft. After all, as competitive as they are in the game, it is, to them, secondary to the real competition of keeping their kites operational.

The crew's zeal encompasses their pilot, with whom they feel an extremely close bond. The pilot has a reciprocal feeling towards his crew, his life is in their hands every time he takes off. The crews are extremely appreciative of pilots who, even after a tough mission, will stay around to test-hop a plane in order to certify to its being airworthy, the final approval for inclusion on the availability roster. This must be done any time a plane has been "Redlined" for mechanical or damage problems. It is impossible to overstate the "Esprit de Corps" and total dedication of these men to the demanding job of keeping "Their" kites operational.

As the mission drones steadily onward, ever closer to the heartland of Germany, the pilots can no longer afford the luxury of even fleeting thoughts of home, wives, or girlfriends. All senses must be focused on the dangerous business at hand. Rendezvous with and protection of the bombers, and personal performance and survival are the consuming thoughts appropriate at this time. There is no time for anything else; a string of past casualties attests to this fact.

A jolt of adrenaline courses through my veins as radio silence is shattered by an anxious voice announcing, "Bogies at ten o'clock high." All senses are instantly directed to the suspect quadrant of the sky as all throttles are pushed to the stop, and the planes begin to climb for the all-important advantage of altitude. Nervous fingers search for the release handle for the external tanks in case the "Bogies" should be recognized as "Bandits." A terse report indicates the "Bogies" are P-38s, attested by their distinctive twin booms, heading home from their segment of the day's mission.

From this point on, there is no relief from the tension of the continual vigil of searching every corner of the sky. Every cloud is suspect of harboring enemy planes, and every glint of reflected sunlight signals the possibility of a lurking Hun prepared to pounce at any instant. To an optimist, each shadow represents a potential combat victory, an opportunity to prove his personal worth to himself and his peers; conversely each pessimist could view this as a step closer to the end of his career or even his life. A new pilot looks for the opportunity to test himself, an older more experienced pilot hopes for one more "Kill" to add to the display of swastikas painted on the cowl of his kite. Although these men fly as part of a Squadron, a part of the Group, each one has an individual burning desire to be the best and stand the tallest in his tight circle of aggressive associates.

Suddenly, garbled chatter on the radio directs attention to the fact that the Group is nearing the rendezvous point with the bombers. The continued tense outbursts indicate there is enemy involvement as the bombers near the target. This is the time of most danger as enemy fighters and flak-gunners co-ordinate to destroy as many of our bombers as possible. When the bombers settle into the steady flight path necessary to set up the bombsights and calculate the bomb drop zone, they can no longer take evasive action. They then present themselves as predictable steady targets for both fighters and flak. The enemy fighters attack relentlessly until the last moment and then as the final bomb run begins, they move out of the area, and the flak-gunners blanket the drop zone with a lethal box barrage of heavy exploding flak. Once the flak subsides, the fighters again move in to harass the formation and to "Kill" any strays or damaged bombers.

Our work is cut out for us as we protect the bombers during the critical approach to the drop zone and beat back the enemy fighters who are attempting to destroy them. As the flak starts in earnest, we withdraw, continuing to fight the enemy, away from the drop area, and then re-enter the bomber defense to keep the Huns from attacking the bombers as they reorganize and start back towards their bases. As other fighters arrive to take over the escort duty, on the bombers return route, we protect the crippled stragglers to keep them from being picked off by the German fighters. These are the critical phases of our escort missions.

Gradually, in the distant haze, tiny black specks slowly materialize into a huge gaggle of B-17s grinding along in tight defensive formation, right on time and right on course. The rendezvous is witness to the skill of the many people involved, a thousand miles from base, over enemy territory, covered most of the way by impenetrable clouds, and accomplished by many different units. They depart at different times and travel at different speeds. The fighters rendezvous at predetermined locations at scheduled times and provide continuous cover for the bombers from their take-off to their return landing.

It soon becomes painfully clear that there are those waiting who want our mission to be anything but successful. A large number of smaller aircraft are diving towards the bombers like a nest of angry hornets.

Over the radio we hear, "This is Horseback, drop your babies and let's get the bastards." Immediately, the nearby sky is full of jettisoned external wing tanks, and all throttles are jammed to the fire wall. Gun switches on, the formation tightens up as with one thought, the Group charges headlong towards the now identifiable Me-109s, and we try to maneuver between them and the bombers, their targets of choice.

Within seconds, the air is full of fighters scrambling in all directions with no further semblance of formation. Now all concerned are motivated by one basic instinct; survival! There are now primarily basic units of two, a unit leader and his wingman in each, inseparable as each protects the other's rear from attack, meanwhile attacking the enemy at any opportunity. The radio is alive with urgent, raucous chatter, "Break left, break left," "Get that son of a bitch off my tail!" "Let's get that Bastard." The air is full of planes, buzzing in every direction, each trying to get a tactical advantage over an enemy plane, we as well as they.

I'm flying Kid Hofer's wing when suddenly a 109 peels across in front of us, and we turn our every attention to him. We quarter in behind him, and whichever way he turns, one of us is in position to fire on him. We take turns firing short bursts as he maneuvers to escape. The hits take their toll as he begins to lose power and a final burst by Hofer produces a trail of smoke. His canopy flies off, and he goes over the side, his chute opening almost as soon as he clears his tail. There, not 50 feet to the side of me, he hangs under his huge white canopy, resplendent in his uniform, his medals clearly visible on his chest, and the sun glinting off his highly polished black knee-high boots. As I roar past him, he smiles and waves, a salute to the victors. He can well smile since he is over his homeland, and tomorrow he'll be up again in another plane. That is a far different fate than would await us were the tables turned.

I can't resist looking down at my own rather grungy-looking coveralls and my much-used A-2 jacket, and scruffy combat boots. I think to myself, "Can you believe the audacity of two such casually dressed pilots, like Hofer and me, that we could be so presumptuous as to shoot down an enemy who is dressed like he is about to lead a parade?" I will never forget the sun glinting off his highly-polished boots.

As we climb back up to altitude, the lack of radio chatter indicates the fight is over or has moved out of our range. A call on the radio produces no useful information as to where our Group is. It is difficult to understand how one moment the sky can be so full of planes, roaring in all directions, with collision a constant danger, and suddenly a moment later the sky is absolutely empty. The fact is, with the speed and violent maneuvers of aerial combat, members of the Group can quickly become separated by miles of sky. As so often is the case, poor visibility contributes to make it practically impossible to rejoin other elements of your Group or Squadron after an episode of intense combat.

What generally happens when two large groups of enemy fighters engage, the planes split off in all directions as they engage individual or small groups of enemy planes in two-on-two or two-on-one combat. Others become engaged in a tight, "Lufbery" circle, where each plane is unable to turn tight enough to get a lead on an enemy plane, likewise, the enemy planes are unable to turn tight enough to get a lead on our planes. During this maneuver, all planes rapidly lose altitude as the aerodynamics of the maneuver rob the wings of lift, and the circle drops lower and lower until the planes eventually have to split off in level flight in order to keep from crashing into the ground.

Our mission completed, with no hope of joining our Group, there is nothing to do but head back to base. Our ammo is an unknown quantity, and we do not have an abundance of fuel. Nevertheless, with Hofer, as with me, there is always a chance of targets of opportunity on the way.

As we cruise along, ever-alert for the enemy, I see a shadow at 10 o'clock low, miles away, near some wispy clouds. That's all it is, but keen eyesight is the most important attribute of a fighter pilot, and you trust your eyes sometimes when your brain does not completely resolve a clear image. In any event, I communicate my "sighting" to Hofer. He sees nothing but says, "Let's have a look, lead the way." As he falls into position on my wing, we open up and head for the distant clouds. Sure enough, as we get closer, there is a B-17 ducking in and out of the skimpy clouds followed by what appears to be two FW-190s firing at it. As we close, we can see the 17's guns blinking like Christmas lights as it defends itself against the attackers. We come barreling down out of the sun, driving up the ass of the 190s. I have the rear one in my sights and am beginning to squeeze the trigger when suddenly I shout, "Break!" and pull wildly to the side as we zoom past the now clearly defined P-47s with their checkered noses gleaming in the sun. Our speed carries us past them, we make a vertical turn to go back and investigate, but by now all planes have disappeared again. We buzz around for some minutes without success, and being low on fuel, we sadly head back to our base. We will never know who were the good guys and who were the bad guys in that encounter. The Germans pulled all sorts of cute little tricks during the European conflict. They rebuilt all kinds of allied aircraft for study and for intrusion into our forces on missions. Sometimes, they would fly a B-17 up to join a crippled B-17 and then attempt to shoot it down, or use one of our rebuilt fighter planes for the same purpose. I learned early in the game never to turn into a U.S. bomber without expecting to see their 50 calibers start twinkling. I had it happen more than once when in formation if the Group swept closer than the bombers found comfortable. I can't say that I blame them.

We roared along toward England hoping for the sight of a train or barge or anything of military value to attack. With the limited visibility, unfortunately, we saw nothing and as we approached the Channel, we climbed back up to avoid the patient gunners who so zealously guard the entrance to the Continent. Apparently, we were an unworthy target, since they didn't waste even one burst of flak on us as we headed out over the Channel toward our base at Debden. Our arrival was uneventful and spirits were high as the debriefing disclosed that hunting had been good and almost everyone had engaged the enemy with no casualties on our part. Of even more importance to me, I had engaged in battle and had not flinched. I now felt I belonged.

This was the 1st of May, and my fifth mission.

Chapter IV

WE SIGHT THE ENEMY

It seemed to have been ages between my graduation from Aviation Cadet School and the occasion of my first mission. The graduation took place on the 1st of October, 1943. After a short leave we spent a week at Dale Mabry in Florida, where the Officers' Mess provided meals that I believe were designed to encourage us to welcome combat duty. A consensus would have indicated that "K" rations would have been preferred.

Once the powers that be, at Dale Mabry, decided what to do with us, we were sent to Bartow Air Base in Florida for our transition training. There, we first encountered the beautiful P-51s. We had thought our 10 hours in P-40s was heaven, but the P-51s soon relegated the 40s to a much lesser spot in our devotion. We now had a plane that could climb beyond our wildest imagination and not drop like a bullet once the nose fell below the horizon. It flew like the AT-6 would if it were supercharged; a real pilot's plane, responsive to your every desire. Due to the needs of combat, we had no surplus planes, and flight time in the 51s was less than we would have wanted, but we did become fairly proficient in the handling of this wonderful plane. The training group found enough tasks to keep us moderately busy for an interminable length of time. It was not until the 1st of February that we finally shipped out to the P.O.E. (Port of Embarkation) for our "Cruise" to England.

Prior to our shipping out to the P.O.E., a very close buddy of mine, Joe Stager, from Long Island, had gotten married. Between us, we managed to rent a two-bedroom furnished apartment in Bartow. There we got our first real introduction to a moving carpet of the kind that was all too familiar in southern States at the time.

The first night, after moving in all of our worldly goods, namely our suitcases, our wives cooked a scrumptious meal, and we ate in. Shortly after eating and doing the dishes, Joe and Maura, being newly married, and Marge and I, just recently reunited, found ourselves very tired, and we all headed for the sack. As we lay quietly, just anticipating subsequent activities, the normal kissing, hugging, and what not was interrupted by a skittering noise. The noise, tentative at first, grew in intensity to the point it demanded investigation. I quietly reached over, turned on the bed-lamp, and we were absolutely dumbfounded at what we saw. The floor was covered with inch-long cockroaches, apparently involved in drag races or some other kind of athletic meet. Their speed was unbelievable as they scampered in all directions and almost instantaneously disappeared as if the light were a pistol shot starting a marathon.

This was our first encounter and provided us with a clue to handling the problem. From then on, all clothing, luggage, etc., was kept on chairs or tables, and a light burned continuously. We also kept a baseball bat handy in case an unusually large one should suddenly appear. Needless to say, the landlord received a visit the next day, and he was totally "surprised" to hear that such a vile colony was cohabiting with us.

As newly commissioned Officer Pilots, this is the way we lived our short moments of happiness, sandwiched in between assignments. Nothing had changed from our tenure as Aviation Cadets. We still took orders from Sergeants; they, after all, were the only ones who knew anything about what was going on. We moved to a new post approximately every three months, and we tried to set up a semblance of a household at each new assignment. Each time we moved, we uprooted our meager belongings, said farewell to our current friends, lost some of our buddies to washout and reassignment, and went into housekeeping again for another transitory period. Our only constants were our desire to be together and our knowledge that each move brought our togetherness closer to an end, and that we needed to make the most of it while we could.

Soon we learned that our next destination would be the P.O.E. at Camp Kilmer on Long Island. We were fortunate in that Joe was able to make arrangements for the four of us to stay at a friend's vacant apartment in New York, just a short subway ride from Kilmer. Of course, everything hinged on our being able to leave the P.O.E., where we theoretically would be "locked-in." Since our departure date was a secret, we arranged with our wives, that, should we not show up any evening or not call, they should immediately head for the prearranged rendezvous point, and we would attempt to communicate with them at the earliest opportunity.

Without notice, we soon entrained for Kilmer and, upon arrival, were sealed in with no communication with the outside world except by censored mail. The "sealing-in" process was not entirely effective for the two of us, having normal young men's desires and very ingenious minds. Knowing that our wives were only a short subway ride away, it took us only two days to develop a strategy to evade the usual controls, and we spent every subsequent night with our wives in the "Big Apple."

We had a grand time seeing Broadway shows, mostly gratis, and dining out. Then we snuggled with our wives until the early alarm clock call sent us running for the subway. Of course, we had, with the complicity of a couple of friends, set up an early warning system wherein they would call us in the event anything surprising would arise. As a consequence, we missed no inspections or troop movements that involved us. The only mishap I encountered was when one morning I fell asleep on the subway and missed my station. I ended up at Coney Island and really had to scramble to get back to base in time for morning check-in.

We were not particularly afraid of being apprehended in our evasion of regulations, since about the worst punishment we could envision was to be shipped overseas. Knowing that was our immediate destination regardless, we ignored the P.O.E. rules with impunity, except, of course, the ones concerning security, which we honored faithfully.

Finally, on the 1st of March, we were rousted out, loaded onto trucks, and were transported to the dock; our absence that evening clearly told our wives that the honeymoon was over and they might as well head for home.

We embarked on a small English ship, HMS *Arawa*, which obviously had some far different duties in a former life. Every available spot had been fitted with a bunk or hammock to accommodate servicemen. There seemed to be a shortage of everything, including room, toilets, showers, chairs, etc. Even the deck space was crowded with all kinds of gear stowed wherever there was a space available to lash it down.

The officers were crowded into double-decked bunks placed against the four walls of the small low-ceilinged staterooms. Their gear was crammed into every available space furthering the claustrophobic effect of the rooms.

This was first class, however, compared to the hull full of soldiers crammed below decks in the windowless, airless belly of the ship. There they endured the constant stench of vomit and the proximity to the many seasick men, too sick to even care about the discomfort of their comrades. Their agony was interrupted only by their infrequent exercise periods on deck or their "Abandon ship" drills.

The trip was a low-grade disaster; the ship was small enough to fit into the depression between each series of swells. The North Atlantic, in winter, has never been known for its kindness to travelers thereon, and it made no exceptions during the horrible two weeks that followed. From the moment that we hit the open sea until our landing in Wales, we lived on an elevator that rose and fell regularly a distance of approximately forty feet from apogee to perigee. If you can imagine a person standing on the *dock* getting seasick, as did happen, imagine the effect this movement had on the hundreds of troops crowded onto this tiny vessel. The mop crews never rested.

I, like most of the pilots, was not affected by this movement. We had survived training in PT-19s in the summer thermals "deep in the heart of Texas." Those who had to wash the noon meal, complete with yellow or red pudding, off their blue, open cockpit planes, after the afternoon flight session, were soon cured or ultimately "washed-out." We lost a good many of our Cadet friends this way as they were reassigned to duties of a less demanding nature.

The up and down motion of the boat, was unsettling enough but the North Atlantic was not satisfied with such a meager display of motion. It provided rocking motions, both sideways, and fore and aft. Walking had never been such a complex movement; it called for all the skills of an advanced equilibrium and superb co-ordination. Sleeping took on a new dimension, with sideboards on the bunks, to keep us from being precipitously ejected during some of the ship's more complex movements.

Standing on deck, with the ship in a trough, I could look up and see indigo-colored water high above me in a 360 degree horizon. In the next instant, the ship would be on the tip of a swell, and I was able to look down on every ship in the convoy. The long tankers, with "cocooned" P-51s lashed to their decks took on the appearance of surfacing submarines as they plowed through, not over the waves. This very different approach looked smooth but not too encouraging to anyone who might fancy a walk on deck. As our ship reached the apogee of a wave, it appeared that the bow and the stern would be out of the water simultaneously, and the engine would surge as the propellers grabbed at non-existent water, and then slowed as the ship sank, back into the normal running position.

Eating was also an interesting procedure. We ate in shifts, food, which was taken from British fare, such as fish, daily, kidney pie, and other somewhat dubious offerings. It was unusual to us but quite nutritious. The plates were kept from sliding off the tables by two-inch high boards around the periphery of the table. The food was bland and not very appetizing but was the least of our concerns during the voyage. The highlight of the culinary day was the famous British custom of "Tea" in the afternoon. This was so utterly out of place, with delicious scones or crumpets and steaming hot tea, as to make one wonder how such diverse offerings could come from the same galley. We looked forward to it with great anticipation.

After a seeming eternity, we docked in Wales and placed our feet on some very welcome but very soggy terra firma. From there, we pilots were shipped by train to the 496 OTU Group for combat operational training. After another endless month, we finally went to our "permanent assignments." I, happily, with my classmates Preston Hardy, Aubrey Hewatt, and Pete Kennedy, was assigned to the 4th Fighter Group, and eagerly looked forward to our arrival on the 17th of April, 1944. It had been an unbelievably long five months since graduation from cadets to this assignment, but now the long wait was about to end.

We began what appeared to be yet another endless preparation with long hours of practice of fundamentals and evasive tactics. We spent more hours reading bulletins and tech orders on tactics and plane performance characteristics. Then came the demanding squadron Balboas. They started with high-level, then very dangerous low-level formation flying, winding through the green hills of England on the deck. We flew so close, I could see the face of our squadron leader, Captain Mike Sobanski. He was the old man of the squadron, a tough taskmaster who would accept nothing short of perfection. His critical eye saw everything, and his terse commands were followed religiously and immediately. The perfection he demanded was the key to ultimate survival; no one questioned that philosophy.

The 4th Group was geared to thinking, living, and being number one, and all preparations were aimed at that goal. Anyone not feeling equal to the attainment of that concept had better be assigned elsewhere; there was just no alternative.

The acceptable performance capabilities were clearly pointed out to us on the first day of our assignment to this Group. All indoctrination stressed the urgency of being aggressive and professional, but nothing was more direct than the short welcoming speech by Col. Don Blakeslee, Group Commander. In summation, he said, "Men, welcome to the 4th Fighter Group. You have been assigned here after completing your training in the 3rd Air Force. There you were required to comply with a myriad of rules, regulations, and orders, governing your conduct in the air and on the ground. These requirements were designed to promote safety for you and your fellow flyers during your training period. Now you are trained combat fighter pilots assigned to a top Fighter Group, in the 8th Air Force. We have the same rules, but we are capable and aggressive, and you must be also. To this end, whenever you leave this base on a flight, do not return to land without breaking some of those rules. BUT DON'T GET CAUGHT, or you will never fly with this Group again! Secondly, if anyone "prangs a kite while stunting, he's out!"

This kind of invitation was the only encouragement necessary to make any aggressive pilot eminently aggressive from that day forward. Needless to say, the selection techniques, the intensive training, and the indoctrination in assertiveness, created pilots with both ability and desire to prove themselves in combat. After all, that's what this was all about. The opportunity to prove oneself, however, still had additional pre-requisites to be mastered.

Our introduction to our Squadron Commander was the next step in our learning just what these tasks were to be. We subsequently were presented to Mike Sobanski, Squadron Commander of 334 Squadron for further enlightenment on what was to be expected of us. Mike was a handsome man, slim yet athletic build, with a hesitant smile, preceded by a disarming glint in his eye when he sparingly indicated approval. Conversely, a slightly ominous spark preceded a frown when he expressed disapproval, and was immediately followed by a rebuke for any misdeeds. Under his tutelage, it was to be what seemed an interminable length of time until the Squadron Commander felt, without ques-

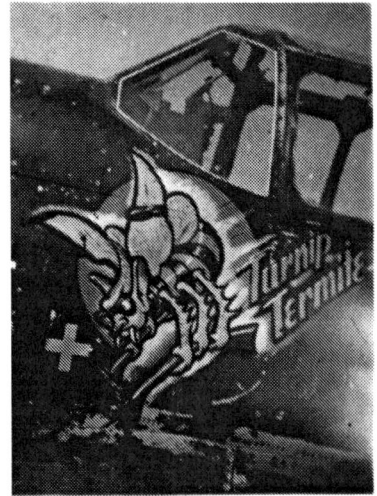

Upper left-"Turnip Termite," inspired by the legendary insects that annually devastated "Dogpatch" in the "Lil Abner" comic series, stands ready to take on the Luftwaffe.
Upper right and lower left-Escape photos carried in combat by all pilots for use in counterfeiting passports or ID papers if downed and picked up by friendly forces. Lower right-Official 4th Fighter Group identification photo.

tion, that your abilities were not only all *you* thought they were but also met *his* demanding standards. You master yourself, your plane, and then you have a chance to master the enemy. Only then would he assign you to go on even a "Milk Run" mission. Then, if your conduct proved acceptable to him, he might assign you to fly on a mission where you could conceivably encounter an enemy plane. Only skilled and responsible pilots were sent into combat with the 4th. Good pilots were scarce, but good planes were even more scarce and more difficult to replace, so the return of both from a mission was strongly encouraged.

Here we were introduced to the "Real Mustangs!" They were equipped to fight, with guns, bomb racks, and wing tanks, whatever the mission demanded. These beautiful Mustangs mounted the devastating firepower of six 50-caliber machine guns with their fire converging at 250 yards. With armor-piercing incendiary ammunition, the results were awesome. They could deliver an annihilating load of hot lead wherever you were capable of directing it. To direct it, required unusual skills. Simultaneously, you had to have your controls coordinated, your target in your crosshairs, or lead calculated appropriately, and to be in range. These criteria were anything but easy to achieve, considering that you could be traveling at upwards of 400 miles per hour, in a vehicle capable of moving in three different planes simultaneously, and shooting at a target with the same multidirectional and speed capabilities. In addition, you had to be able to detect your enemy's attempts to deceive your perception of his true course by introducing a little yaw, or sideways motion, which would make you believe he was going in a slightly different direction than you perceived it to be. Once all these criteria were met, the firepower of the 51s was capable of literally chewing an enemy plane to pieces. Against a ground target, such as a train, anyone having the misfortune of being caught in the 51's sights, could count on being demobilized, often accompanied by billowing geysers of white steam as the screaming half-inch diameter bullets blasted the hot boiler of the engine.

All of this information absorption, and all of this flight training is interesting, but the constant gnawing question is always, "When are we going to see action?" We started a continuous training routine when we arrived on the 17th, and we felt we were missing all the action. On the 18th, on a Berlin mission, the Group destroyed 19 enemy planes for a loss of three. Mike, unfortunately had an electrical system problem and had to abort. On the 19th, six more were destroyed, and one lost on a mission to Eschwege. Mike led the Group with Kolter, Hofer and Hills in his Flight. They met the bombers OK and then they were bounced by 75 to 100 FW-190s and Me-109s. Mike remarked he had never seen such a big gaggle; he was bounced time and again but was not hit. He clobbered the hell out of an Me-109 and saw him hit the deck. He took a picture of him before returning to base. Anderson, of 335 took a squirt at a P-51 from another Group, by mistake, without his gunsight, but fortunately stopped in time.

On the 20th, Mike led the Group again, to Paris, in what he called a typical "stooge show," where he was vectored to all sorts of friendly aircraft. He stated, "Not a goddam thing seen; brought a few Forts out near Dieppe."

Also, on the 20th, something new was added. Liquid-filled "G" suits arrived, and we were directed to fly five hours of practice in these abominable sets of rubber underwear. The theory was great. The suit, with a series of lacings, was fitted tightly to a pilot's legs, abdomen, and chest. After this customizing, it could be removed or put on by use of appropriate zippers. When in use, bladders in the chest area were filled with water. When a high-G pullout occurred, the water, being heavier than blood, was pulled by gravity, through unidirectional restriction valves and tubes, into bladders behind the calves and over the abdomen. This prevented the blood from migrating to the lower extremities and thus starving the eyes and brain, causing "blackout."

This equipment did a marvelous job, allowing pilots to pull up to 10 "G's," from a normal 5 or 6 "G's," for limited periods of time, without blacking out. Theoretically, we might be able to tear the wings off a plane before blacking out! Unfortunately, no provision had been made for the release of this pressure, once the mechanism had been activated. The result was that the water in the leg bladders completely shut off the supply of blood to the legs and feet causing excruciating pain to these extremities as you continued to fly, and the pain increased the longer you flew.

The intensity of this pain caused many to carry a knife to stab the lower bladders of the "G" suit, releasing the water, which in turn, relieved the pressure to the calves and allowed the blood to return, bringing blessed relief to the pilot. Unless you could return quickly to base and remove the suit, this was the only alternative, otherwise, the pain made it impossible to concentrate on flying. Of course, this action was an unacceptable alternative, "destroying Government property," and resulted in the suits never being used in combat.

On the 22ND, over Kassel-Hamm, 17 more enemy planes "bit the dust," with Willard Millikan accounting for four 109s himself, with a loss of one pilot. Mike, leading the top-cover squadron, got a high-deflection shot at a 109, which he damaged but did not down. Prior to this mission, Mike led his squadron in a Balboa. After an hour of practice, Mike saw fit to enter in his log "New boys not too bad; will need a bit more polishing though; some jerk in 335 made me go around in the circuit; could've murdered the bastard, I was so mad."

That same day, a directive came from Col. Blakeslee, to the effect that we would now be flying from dawn to dusk, especially the newer pilots, in preparation for the "busy" season. This was followed on the 23rd with another memo laying down "Ground Rules" that required the wearing of proper uniforms, saluting, participating in PT, and being prompt for duty assignments, among other things. That night, we flew practice until after midnight.

Eventually, it all came together on the 24th of April. Two noteworthy things had happened; the orders assigning 6 of us to the 4th Group as of 17 April, and I went on my first mission. I had the security of flying on Captain Sobanski's wing as he led the 334th Squadron. It was almost like one of the major check-rides in Aviation Cadet School. Lt. Markel and my friend Lt. Don Malmsten comprised the other element of our Flight. The mission was Freelance Support for bombers with Munich as their target. Needless to say, I had butterflies all the way. Finally, all my training was coming to fruition; would I be up to it? Fortunately, it turned out to be a good mission for getting my feet wet. Sobanski aborted due to blower trouble. (Later he admitted in his diary, "Finger well up! Mistook 17,000 for 27,000, thought my blower wouldn't work, Silly)." The spare, Lt. Siems, joined the Flight, with me flying Lt. Markel's wing. Next Siems developed engine trouble and headed home with Lt. Malmsten accompanying him. That left Markel and me as the only ones remaining in our White Section. The Group ran into 34 FW190s and Me109s near Worms, and in the ensuing battle, I could do little but stay with Markel and keep out of trouble. I was totally unprepared for the melee that ensued, with planes scrambling in all directions. None of our section got off a shot, but the Squadron claimed three 190s, and one 109 destroyed, and one 190 damaged for some really good hunting by Lts. Pierce, Megura, and Howe, all seasoned pilots. The rest of the Group accounted for 13 more Krauts. We reported one casualty, Lt. Biel, MIA.

On the 26th we had an uneventful Sweep to Trier which was followed later by a practice bombing mission.

On 27 April, flying as the spare, I filled in the #3 slot to Lt Megura when Lt Lang aborted with a malfunctioning prop. The Mission took us to Dunkirk.

Then Mike led the Group on a trip to Berlin, on the 29th, resulting in seven enemy destroyed with two of ours lost. The two lost on this mission were both friends of mine who had been assigned to the 4th with me; Pete Kennedy and John Barden. This left only four of us from the original six who had arrived together. We had been assigned on the 17th of April. All of the training they had completed was lost with only 12 days in the Group prior to becoming POWs.

On the 30TH, I finally, after a couple of uneventful missions, got to fly on a mission with some action, as Lt. Montgomery's wingman, strafing Lyon/Brou airfield. Even if you don't have the opportunity to shoot at a plane, strafing an airdrome can be extremely hazardous to your health. The Germans were very strongly attached to their aircraft and defended their airdromes with hundreds of small-bore weapons, which they never hesitated to use. Mike shared in the destruction of an Me-110 and damaged another but got his kite badly shot up in the process. He was really "sweating out" his return to England with two Oxy bottles popped and his coolant door inoperative. After he returned, he was quoted as saying "A shakey do, I'm an Ace now!" In any event, there was enough excitement and enough fuel consumed to force some of us to land prematurely at East Wretham to refuel after 5 ½ hours of flight.

This day's destruction of five Huns edged the Group over the mark of 500 E/A destroyed. (On 29 July, the seven week score in March and April, which stood at 323 E/A destroyed, was recognized by the award of the 4th's first "Distinguished Unit Citation"). Unfortunately, this achievement cost the Group the loss of 44 pilots and planes during that same period. Simple arithmetic indicates the danger of our occupation by concluding that at that rate, the entire pilot complement would be turned over every three months. Of course, this does not mean me: I am invulnerable! I wonder how many POWs were pondering that philosophy right then!

Although I had not contributed, the month's hunting had raised the Group's total to 505½ enemy planes destroyed as of the end of April. This, of course, was cause for a celebration, and the party was long and hearty. Celebrations were another activity that the 4th handled capably. With its record of successes, there were many parties and many celebrations, and it soon became a reason for more and more dignitaries to just happen to be in the area and drop in for these parties.

As the Spring weather became more stable, mission activity was picking up.

On the 7th of May, I went on my first trip to Berlin, my first "Ops" in the "Turnip Termite." Greatly anticipated, it turned out to be a tremendous disappointment. There was 10/10ths cloudcover and no enemy aircraft arose to greet us. There was just intense flak over the target, which really offered no enticement to anyone.

On the next day, we got a return visit to Berlin. Mike again led 334 Squadron while I ended up as a spare. About an hour into the mission, Mike developed stomach cramps and had to turn back. Prior to that, three others had aborted so I ended up leading a Section consisting of Hardy, Howe and myself,

After our escort duties were relieved by a group of P-47s, we broke off north of Dummer Lake and headed back toward base. North of the Ruhr, we came upon a straggling B-17 being attacked by four enemy fighters. The three of us in my Section immediately dove and attacked the E/A with guns blazing, severely damaging at least two of them. They quickly dove into the clouds and we were unable to find them again. As so often happens, under severe weather conditions, our later gun-camera assessment showed nothing but haze, so the final outcome was inconclusive.

I continued to search for the Huns without results, and when I broke out below the clouds, I discovered that I was alone, having lost my wingman in the dense clouds. Since I was unable to raise anyone on the radio, I headed back towards the base. As usual, I looked for and found a stray bomber, too wounded to keep up with its Group, and escorted it towards England. As we continued, the clouds increased in density to the extent that I could no longer safely escort the bomber. I felt it now had good enough cover to continue alone and would have only radar-directed flak with which to contend. I was very apprehensive about the fact that I soon encountered clouds so thick that I had to rely solely on instruments. I picked up a heading of 270 degrees, and when I figured I was surely over the edge of the English Channel, I switched to the emergency channel, made sure my IFF was on, and called for a fix. After proper identification, I was instructed to fly a heading of 270 degrees at an indicated air speed of 320 miles per hour, for twenty minutes, and then start letting down at the rate of five hundred feet per minute. The controller said that I should break out of the crud at four-to-five hundred feet over the Channel and that I could then stay under the overcast and feel my way back to the coast, on a visual basis, and land at a forward air base. Of course, I believed every word he said, without question.

I had called for a barometer reading and had reset my altimeter to the current pressure. I let down as directed, until my altimeter was below two hundred feet. I then felt that my altimeter was not correct or that something else was amiss. In order to preclude the possibility of an unseasonable swim, I started to let down at a slower speed and cut back my air speed to two hundred and fifty miles per hour. I was letting down as if I were trying to land on eggs. My eyes were straining to see the water below; would it never appear, or was I to crash into it and become a casualty of the air war with a footnote in some squadron diary "Lt. Frank Speer, crashed in the Channel, KIA"?

Hitting that water, at that speed, even two-fifty, would be like hitting a brick wall. Neither the plane nor I could survive the impact. Slowly, ever so slowly, I literally felt my way down, foot by interminable foot. Suddenly, there it was not fifty feet below my wings, looking darkly gray, ominous and threatening, as if laying menacingly in wait for me hoping I would make even the slightest mistake. I was determined, at that point, to beat the Channel that had claimed so many flyers, and to rewrite the final paragraph.

Thinking this, however, was far from ending my ordeal. The fifty feet was a temporary illusion. The clouds hung down like curtains, here touching the water, there, leaving a fifty-foot clearance from the water, in some places, only ten to twenty feet. Flying into the curtain, there was no guarantee that I would break out the other side into a clearing. In fact, just the opposite was more common. It was definitely not for the faint of heart. That impervious looking body of water took on a personal note as it patiently waited to claim me as its next victim and add my name to its long list of conquests.

Another fix indicated that I was on a course for the Thames Estuary where I should not expect to run into any buildings. Suddenly, a vague shape loomed ahead out of the fog. I hauled back on the stick as my instincts shouted, "Shit, a battleship!" and I expected at any second to be the target of a wall of flak and metal. As I zoomed over the object, much to my relief, I saw it was one of the gun emplacements on stilts stuck in the estuary bed, guarding the approach to London. Fortunately, they did not fire, or I would have been a dead duck.

This obstacle passed, here again, I was at 500 feet in the impenetrable clouds, and had to again feel my way down to sea level. By now, I was as wet from sweat as if I had been in the Channel itself. The tension was so intense, it was like a weight around my neck. Adding to my serious problems with the weather, I now was getting dangerously low on fuel. Slowly, I inched down, this time I was a little more lucky than last, breaking out at about one hundred feet, but immediately facing another curtain of rain and clouds. I dropped down further and flew so low that I occasionally sent spray backwards from my prop wash, I edged forward straining for any sight of land.

My eyes felt like sandpaper from the strain of the constant search for the slightest glimpse of terra-firma. Then it appeared, and with it a minute respite, as the clouds over the land seemed to offer just a minuscule bit more clearing in which to fly. The relief was short-lived, as even the lowliest hill had its peak shrouded in the dense and forbidding cloud. At least, over the Channel there were no hidden hills with which to cope. It now became a study in flying in the valleys or slight depressions between the low hills with the hope that there would not be any sudden unexpected encounters of a fatal nature. The stress was now a little less severe since I no longer had to fly on instruments, and I now had the unsavory option of pulling up and bailing out if no other alternatives presented themselves.

To find an airfield in this part of England should not be too much of a problem since just about any level piece of land, large enough for a runway, was an airdrome. These forward fields were ringed with the cadavers of formerly beautiful planes that had found their final resting places on a wing and a prayer. There off to the left, a glimpse of a field with a familiar type of camouflaged building gave a great burst of energy to my, by now, exhausted body. A shallow turn and a direct approach soon ended the harrowing experience. I could have kissed the ground in relief, but settled for a silent thanks to the One who had guided me safely to that glorious spot. As usual, a convoy of security personnel, fire trucks and "meat wagons" was there to greet me. It certainly was a gratifying sight to behold, and it was great to know that I did not need them. They invited me to their mess hall for dinner with them, and after a comfortable night, my kite having been refueled, I took off early the next day for Debden. It was a routine trip, and I was warmly welcomed by my Crew-Chief and my pilot friends.

I couldn't help but marvel at the similarity of this event to the one related by Mike concerning his third flight in a Spitfire. He was training at #57 O.T.U. in Hawarden, North Wales in February, a notoriously bad weather month. He was authorized to familiarize himself with the handling of the Spit by doing all kinds of stalls; power on, power off, flaps down, etc. Tiring of this after determining that it was easy to anticipate a stall, "She shivers like a madman but doesn't drop a wing like a Harvard used to do," he decided to try a spin, even though he had been cautioned that they were forbidden without advance permission. "Well it's all bullshit! A Spit only takes half a turn to come out of it."

After half a dozen spins, he heard the base recalling all planes due to bad weather. Descending below the clouds, "Here the Hell started," the clouds were getting low, and it was extremely hazy. Mike was unable to recognize any landmarks. He tried a homing but apparently they could not respond. He flew around under the clouds but the ceiling kept getting lower and lower and visibility kept getting worse. He was down to 200 feet and all the towns he flew over looked alike. He followed rivers which led to nowhere and railroads which seemed to proliferate unendingly. He was now down to the bottom half of his bottom tank of fuel and was considering climbing up through the clouds to bail out. He prayed for a field big enough to crash land but they were all small.

With 10 minutes of fuel left, flying very low along a road, he caught sight of a movement and upon investigation, saw it was an Anson that appeared to be landing. Sure enough, it did land at a big aerodrome and Mike followed in the circuit and landed. His fuel was gone, and his glycol was overheating. "Boy was I ever relieved and thankful to God to find that drome. God didn't fail me." It turned out to be a British bomber base way out of his flying area and he was picked up and returned to his base. There he not only endured the kidding of his pilot friends, "Getting lost in the circuit," but he had to confront his C.O. "I went to see Baraldi and take all the shit I deserved. He told me what a bloody fool I was to fly into 10/10 clouds, and that I was damn lucky not to hit any hills or balloon barrages. It wasn't funny watching that gas getting lower and lower either."

During the period, while training to go on Ops, I had to perform one of the more mundane duties required of a fighter pilot: "Slow Time." I was assigned a new plane and told to get it operational. It was a P-51B #436957, Squadron Code QP-M. It was olive drab color, and I immediately named it "Turnip Termite." Turnip Termites had a long history of devastating the community of "Dogpatch," of "Li'l Abner" fame. I thought the name appropriate for a war machine.

The boring part of "Slow Time" is just that: 10 hours of flying at low manifold pressures, (translates to slow speed) with no aerobatics or unusual stresses on the engine. You just grind away, monotonously, hour after hour, totally unlike the normal duty of a fighter pilot.

After completing my required 10 hours, I took the kite up for a real workout; it was disappointing to say the least. The engine ran well but certainly not at top performance. Capt. Sobanski, kept asking me, "When is it going to be ready?" Finally, we discussed the problem at length. He told me to take it up, break the "War Emergency Seal," and run it full-bore for ten minutes, cool it down, and bring it in. I gleefully followed his advice and gave it a real workout. The crew checked the screens, oil, etc., as required, anytime the War Emergency Seal has been broken. Everything being positive, I took it up the next day and was delighted with the results. The engine purred; it was responsive, and I was able to pull an extra 10 to 15 mph, in level flight. I was ecstatic, and my flying showed it. I really had a great time wringing it out.

Meanwhile, I had gotten together with Don Allen, who was our unofficial insignia connoisseur, with the request that he design and paint a "Turnip Termite" on my kite. He admitted that it was quite a challenge, since there was no prototype, such as a shapely woman or other familiar symbol with which to work. Nevertheless, we soon developed the perfect "Turnip Termite." It was a gruesome, greenish-tinged, striped-bodied insect with six ugly appendages wielding two blunderbusses, with two bombs suspended beneath its wings. It was wearing goggles, baring huge incisors, and diving as it fired its guns.

I excitedly sought out Mike and informed him the "Termite was ready."

Meanwhile, I devoted any spare time doing one of the things I liked most doing. I loved to test the planes that needed to be tested before being cleared to go operational. Whenever a plane had any kind of mechanical or physical problem requiring any but routine work, it was redlined, temporarily out of service. Before it could then be sent on another mission, it had to be test flown. This test hop was one of my favorite pastimes, and I gladly did it for anyone whose plane needed testing. It was fun; I could really wring it out. I would take off, climb to altitude, fly around the clouds at full throttle, do a couple of rolls, maybe a loop or two, fly upside down, and then head for the deck. There I would rip along at full speed, flying between trees around hills and experience the thrill of speed like no other available pursuit. Flying at four hundred miles per hour, plus, less than ten feet from the ground, gives a feeling of speed and freedom unknown to probably anyone but a fighter pilot. It is a thrill beyond thrill.

As a grand finale, I would climb to 5,000 or more feet, roll over and dive at the Officer's Club pulling out at the last possible instant, with a chimney shaking roar, pull up and around, and grease it in for a combat type landing.

Frequently, if I had the time, I would soar up to five to ten thousand feet and look around for another fighter. When I was able to find one, we would engage in a real scrambling, turning diving mock dogfight, so thrilling it would make my whole day. I engaged P-38s, P-51s, P-47s, A-20s, and anyone else willing to spend the time on the same thing I was looking for: fun. This can be a dangerous game and came very close to prematurely ending my career as a fighter pilot.

One day, I went for a test hop and had prearranged to meet one of the other pilots for some simulated dogfighting. We had engaged and were scrambling around the sky when we caught sight of two P-38s, apparently doing the same thing we were doing. We teamed up our two P-51s and bounced the 38s. They immediately engaged, if for no other reason than to prove that they could not be outdone by two P-51s. Never having engaged in combat with a twin-engined plane before, we had a good lesson in how they could go into a turn, cut back the power on one engine, and literally fall out of the sky in front of us. This maneuver ended up in a break-off with both elements going away from each other and then turning back towards each other, resulting in a head-on approach. With the speed of each element approaching four hundred miles per hour, we had a passing speed of nearly eight hundred miles per hour, leaving no time for decision making.

We approached each other in tight formation. Suddenly, in milliseconds the thought crossed my mind. "These fellows have the same training as we." The training had always been, if making a head-on pass at a German plane, "Bore right straight at him, he will break." If we bore right at each other, there will be four piles of junk in somebody's pasture along with four bodies of much-needed fighter pilots. In less time than it takes to think about it, my decision was made, at the last instant, drop the nose;

that is the most unlikely maneuver to be made. Accordingly, I popped the stick forward, jamming myself up against the canopy in time to see a P-38 pass inches above me as the second one passed off to my left and my wingman somewhere off to my right.

There followed a moment of silent-thanks, immediately followed by a solemn vow to never again make a head-on pass at a friendly aircraft.

Shaken by this incident, we headed for the base and turned the aircraft over with a clean bill of health. The respective Crew-Chiefs never knew how close they came to having neither plane nor pilot and were happy to have their planes back on combat-ready status.

Even though some of us were now on combat status, during any lull in operations, we were still required to participate in the Squadron Balboas. They never became any easier or less dangerous. One day on a Balboa, with Sobanski, the task-master, leading, I was flying his wing, on a low-level tight formation exercise. He was really hugging the contours of the hills and valleys, and it called for all my skill to stay as tight on his wing as he wanted and to keep an eye on the area in front of me as well. Off to my left was another element of two, facing the same set of challenges. The radio was silent except for Mike's frequent "urgings" to close it up and keep your head moving. An unexpected voice broke in and said, "This is Red Four, would someone check my plane; it is flying rough and the wind screen is covered with something?" A cursory check by the element leader indicated some damage to his wing, and suggested that he return to base.

As Red Four came in to land, he noticed that the plane started to stall at a considerably higher speed than is usual and so he came in under power. Upon landing, he dismounted and looked at his plane. The beautiful Mustang was no longer beautiful. The leading edge of the wing was crushed, in some places back to the main spar, on both wings, utterly destroying the normal airfoil and causing the higher speed stall. The windscreen was covered with sap and bits of leafy material, and to add insult to injury, the air scoop contained a 6-foot piece of tree trunk about 10 to 12 inches in diameter. The evidence showed that he had obviously flown straight through a rather imposing tree and had not even been aware of it. Apparently he had been too intent on watching his section leader and had not been watching where he was flying. All he had to say was that he felt a jolt and then could not see through the windscreen, and that his engine was running rough. He obviously was not in a position to continue to fly low level Balboas at 400 miles per hour.

That night he became exceedingly drunk, and the following day he was nowhere around. He had shipped out, and I never saw him again. To this day, I have no idea of what happened to him. It was evident that Blakeslee meant what he said in his welcoming speech to us.

On one of our infrequent days off, word was passed around that there was an urgent need for some particular parts to get a couple more 51s operational. The parts were available at a depot approximately 150 miles away, and due to the urgency, there was a need for two pilots to volunteer to fly up to the depot to pick up these parts. There was a twin-engined Oxford assigned to the Group, and it was available for the trip. Hofer immediately volunteered, as did I. I had never flown a twin-engined plane before, let alone a British plane, but since there were two pilots and two engines, one engine apiece, I figured I could handle it. Hofer finally admitted that he had never flown a twin either, but he had flown as copilot in this plane once before. We figured if we flew with Hofer, as pilot, and me as copilot, and we took the crew-chief along to take care of the obvious things we needed to do and did not know how to do, we could very easily get the job done. These little necessities were such things as changing gas tanks, raising and lowering the wheels at appropriate times, flap use, etc. The crew-chief was eager to go with us and asked one of his Crew to join us. They considered it a real treat to fly, especially with the opportunity to physically help in the flying process.

We actually got off to an exceptionally good start, due more to the inherent stability and air-worthiness of the plane, than to the skill of the pilot and co-pilot. We headed it down the appropriate runway, fed the throttles evenly, and the plane did the rest, becoming airborne in spite of us. It was a simple plane to fly, being very light, but designed to carry much more load than we were carrying. It was so easy, we took turns flying it and the crew-chief saw to it that we always were using a tank that had gas in it and that we had proper mixture control.

The flight was uneventful; we found the aerodrome with no trouble, thereby proving that navigation fundamentals worked the same whether flying British or American planes. When it came to landing, however, it was an entirely different story. We both were used to the typical combat landing wherein we swooped across the field at low level, pulled up sharply, did a 360 degree climbing turn, cut back on the throttle, then a descending turn, and greased it in with an almost dead engine. With two pilots, unfamiliar with handling two engines and a plane with light wing loading, we elected to do a semi-airline approach from roughly one thousand feet altitude.

We started our letdown from a distance we considered appropriate, leveled our wings, and started to land. Soon it was apparent that we were not descending at a great enough rate. We cut the engine rpm's and lowered a few degrees of flaps but continued to soar. At the point where we should be touching down, we were still at least 500 feet above the runway, and no amount of descent short of a dive would get us near the aerodrome on this approach. We wisely elected to gun the engines and go around for another try. In so doing, with flaps down, we soared skyward at a higher rate than anticipated and found ourselves at an even higher altitude than when we started the first pass.

To counteract this increased altitude, we cut the engine back more than on the first pass and put down twice as many degrees of flaps. As we approached the airdrome, we appeared to be in a good position to land and started to cut back our speed in order to reach touchdown speed. The speed lowered but the plane did not; this time however, we were much closer, being only about 50 feet above the runway when we passed the midpoint. We accordingly gunned the engines, pulled up the wheels and flaps, and went around again. This time we gave ourselves an extra mile to approach and made our letdown farther from the airdrome. We figured to haul it in at low altitude on the engines and then cut them when we approached the end of the runway. Doing just that, believe it or not, we finally touched down and even had a few feet of runway left when, with much braking, we finally rolled to a stop.

We all were greatly relieved when we were finally earthbound. We secured the parts, prepared the plane for take-off for the return journey, and all but I climbed back in. I felt my duty was to be an accomplished fighter pilot and fight the Nazis. In order to do this, I felt discretion was the better part of valor, and in order to be available to do my job, fighting, I elected to take the train back to Debden. It was an enjoyable trip, and the engineer had absolutely no trouble stopping smoothly at the station where I left the train and grabbed a lift to the base.

Word of our little excursion was already making the rounds of the Officers' Club, when I arrived, and it seemed that opinions were split rather evenly as to whether or not my terrestrial return had been an act of cowardice.

On the 9th of May, we awoke to weather that was less than desirable, with the prognostication that it would improve as the day went on. We pulled a real Donnybrook, a Jackpot to St. Dizier. We were to escort the bombers through the target area then attack the aerodrome. Everything started out as planned, but plans sometimes go awry.

Our first mishap occurred as we crossed the invisible line of the coast far below, covered as usual with a normal density of clouds. The anticipated black puffs of smoke told us we were encroaching on the Continental air rights, so jealously guarded by the unseen flak gunners far below. We initiated our mild evasive maneuvers, and everything seemed routine as we continued on our way.

Shortly thereafter, I happened to be looking off to my left and, in the distance, I saw one of our planes, "Tail End Charlie."

He was the farthest plane to the left of the formation, sort of sitting out there all by himself, possibly seven hundred yards away. We were just routinely cruising along, over the clouds, when suddenly there was a huge puff of white smoke, a very unusual color, and when it cleared, there was absolutely no sign of the plane, not even any visible wreckage floating down. It was as if the plane had just disappeared. I never heard anything further of the plane or the pilot, and there was never any official comment or explanation of this phenomenon. Later, I heard of a cryptic entry in the Group log to the effect that a missing pilot had not been seen to go down.

We escorted the bombers over St. Dizier and then dove down and strafed the aerodrome. There was a lot of flak as we made several passes and shot up everything in sight. Flak towers, buildings, planes, and vehicles; all fell prey to our thundering 50 calibers. As if to prove this is a dangerous occupation, we had two planes hit by flak and the pilots had to bail out, Lts. Blanchfield and Burroughs, becoming MIA. My friend and classmate Lt. Sherman also bought it as his prop hit the ground, and he had to crash-land nearby. He too became status, MIA.

On the 10th of May, the Group had a Ramrod to Brunswick, Germany. The show was aborted on the way in, and the Group returned without event.

Two days later, we had a more lively show: this time, bomber escort to Brux. Flying as wingman, I didn't have much to do but hang on for the ride. It was an exciting ride, but I had no opportunity to fire on any targets. However, our Squadron accounted for three kills, adding to the Group total of eleven for the day. Sobanski was disgusted because he had to drop his wing-tanks prematurely on a loused up bounce near Schweinfurt and then missed the fun over the target because he had to head back to base, low on gas.

Weather over the continent and logistical requirements, limited us to two missions during the next eight days. I was not on either of these missions, which resulted in seven more enemy destroyed and two of our pilots downed. During this lull in combat operations the crews busied themselves making alterations to the fuel lines in order to changeover from 75 gallon to 108 gallon wing tanks for greater range.

In the meantime, a new more stringent Station Defense plan went into effect. It was also announced that a new operational tour of three hundred hours would be effective immediately. Due to an increase in avoidable flying and taxiing accidents, those responsible could expect to be fined or grounded in the future.

On the 20th we had an uneventful trip, a Freelance with bombers to Liége. We chased down several reports of enemy aircraft but were unable to make contact and returned to base with no encounters for the day.

On the 21st things again picked up, our Mission was Chattanooga #1. Col. Blakeslee led us out over the Continent, where we had to let down, through holes in the dense cloud cover, as separate Squadrons. We had a real blast, attacking trains, tugs on the Elbe, a radar station, and military vehicles. Lts. Fraser, Hills, Sharp, Hofer, Hewatt, Seims, and I attacked and destroyed four trains. One of the trains apparently was carrying munitions. As I dove on the train, firing at a boxcar, it suddenly blew up right in front of me, sending up huge pieces of debris and shock waves. I had no choice, it was so close, I flew right through it and miraculously, did not even get a scratch as the blast tossed my plane like a toy. It was a frightening experience, but I had no time to dwell on it; there was so much happening.

We turned our attention to an unidentified airdrome that was just begging to be beat-up. Hofer and Hewatt combined to knock down a Bu-131 that was in the pattern trying desperately to land. I was flying on Seims wing. He was a very aggressive pilot, a classmate of mine, and together, we comprised a fearless, or some might say stupid, combination. On our first pass, Seims was concentrating on a couple of Me-210s, and I busied myself firing on a Ju-88, that just happened to be in the way of my gun-sight. The flak was intense, but being "invulnerable," we pressed on, went around, and made a second pass. Seims liked those 210s, so he continued to send them his 50-caliber greetings while I turned my attention to a likely looking Ju-52. On our last pass, we could see two of the 210s burning, and likewise my Ju-88 and Ju-52 were engulfed in smoke and flame. But out of nowhere, the flak gunners must have found my range, for my plane lurched to the right, in a painful move, and I had to turn my attention 100% to flying.

At zero altitude, there is little room for error. I pulled up, just slightly, to keep from hitting the ground, but not high enough to present a better target, and fought the controls to keep my wing up while I desperately juggled trim tabs to bring the controls into equilibrium. In seconds, we were far enough from the field to climb to a more comfortable altitude where I could make final trim tab adjustments and head for home.

I now had an opportunity to look at the cause of my problem, a jagged gash along the outer part of my right wing where a 20 or 37mm shell had peeled back a section of the wing, completely spoiling the airfoil of that segment. Fortunately, it was far enough out that it had not damaged the controls or any of the gas tanks. In lining up the gash on the wing however, it was only too apparent that the shell had missed me by only a few inches, but then as I said before, we were invincible. I thought that maybe I should revise that concept to: "At least I'm damn lucky."

While all of this was happening, Fraser was busily shooting up a pair of Ju-88s. We looked back at the carnage we had created and happily, could see columns of smoke swirling skyward. Since destruction was our business, we felt good about the day's work. On the way back to Debden, the shell hole through my starboard wing, definitely did not improve the aerodynamics of the plane, but we managed to arrive safely back at our base. Although it is of little consolation, I was glad I was not flying the "Turnip Termite" that day because it would then have been "off Ops" for an extended period for repairs.

Mike had a great day; first he received his promotion from 1st Lt. to Captain, and then he got involved in shooting up trains. He said "Bags of fun, shooting up four trains and watching civilians run, our Group got 28 locos and six E/A on the ground."

The next day, the 22nd, back in the "Termite," we took off for a Freelance and escort to Kiel. 336 Squadron broke off to intercept ten Me109s while we continued to escort the bombers. After the bombers left the coast over the North Sea, we attacked 30-plus FW-190s, preventing an attack on the bombers, but we did not score, due to mechanical problems. Capt. Megura's section got into a brawl with some 109s, helped by a number of P-38s. During the ensuing fracas, his plane suffered damage, and he headed for Sweden, where he made a forced-landing and became an internee. Unfortunately for Mike, Megura was flying Sobanski's plane "Mike VI."

On the 23rd, we took off on an escort mission over Chaumont and Troyes. Mike led the Group but I, disappointedly, had to abort due to wing tanks cutting out at altitude, and sadly returned to base without crossing the Channel. Our Group saw no enemy aircraft that day, just more flak.

Chapter V

24 MAY-MISSION BERLIN

The usual preliminaries were behind us, and the form-up and Channel crossing had been boringly uneventful. The engine purred its way towards our distant rendezvous. The monotony was allowing the usual lethargy to set in. Several missions ago, I had lost my farm-boy intensity of entering the field on opening day, shotgun in hand, excitedly expecting a pheasant to fly from the first clump of grass I encountered. Now I do not expect to see a Hun come barreling at me the moment I cross the Channel, but I am cautiously aware that the possibility exists and stay alert as a consequence.

Looking down on the small, puffy white, broken clouds far below, and the seemingly endless blue sky above, there is no sense of motion. It is as though we are drifting along at a snail's pace through some never-ending, slow motion galaxy where time stands still. The warm morning sun fills the cockpit with its bright soothing delight, a far cry from the usual Spring offerings back at the base at Debden.

There, this morning's fare was overcast with diffused sunlight struggling to filter through and alert the occupants of the base that it was indeed daytime. As if to make doubly sure that the residents would not become too preoccupied with the drabness offered, occasional showers punctuated the monotony of this meteorological phenomenon. The night, as if to accentuate the possibility that the day might presume to be too optimistic, was the epitome of drabness. The drabness was confused and made eerie by the fog that enshrouded and imprisoned every visible object in its diffusing grasp. The invidious fog reduced the outdoor world to a circle of, at best, 25 feet in diameter, of subdued darkness with occasional, barely discernible areas where a faint glow defined the attempt of a brave light to fight its way through the foreboding gloom.

The warm sun and the early hour of rising, combine to have a hypnotic effect on the pilots as they struggle to remain alert. I can't help but feel concern for anyone who had the misfortune of staying late at the Officers' Club or of imbibing too much the night before. He is most likely on oxygen right now to help burn off the after-effects. There is not even any radio chatter to help; each one is on his own, in his lonely little glass-enclosed world, with only his own devices to keep him alert. Each knows he, himself, is responsible for his continued well-being as he hurtles along at an indicated air speed of 350 miles per hour, which at that altitude, translates to over 400 miles per hour. At this speed, it takes only a brief period of time to get into serious trouble with any lapse of concentration.

Suddenly, I spot a tiny speck far away and high, and break radio silence: "Cobweb leader, Bogies at two o'clock high." A few seconds of silence, and the command returns, "I don't see them, lead the way." I jamb the throttle to the firewall and lead the way towards the distant object as my element leader falls back to my wing position. Intent only on keeping visual contact with the illusive dots, as they begin to grow larger, I barrel on at full bore climbing steadily to gain the advantage of superior altitude. The dots grow steadily larger and become identifiable as six Me-109s, echelon right, in a gentle turn to the left. At this point, their status becomes "Bandits." Meanwhile, there being twenty or more Bandits visible in the hazy, nearby sky, elements of the Group are breaking off, in appropriate numbers, to attack them, leaving the six first sighted to my wingman and me. As we are approaching from the rear and slightly below, it appears that the enemy, intent on attacking the now visible bombers, is unaware of the impending danger approaching them at 400 miles per hour. There is no emergency tactic, no evasive action, just a continuing gentle turn in towards the distant bombers.

This inattention on their part, is an invitation to disaster and gives me a slight opportunity to take stock of the situation, outnumbered as we are six to two. Check: guns and camera switch on, wing tanks jettisoned, gunsight operational, full power, gas on full fuselage tank, and wingman in position. Six of the enemies' best fighters; how do we survive this one? These thoughts take only milliseconds to sprint through my mind. Another instant and I decide that the lead man of the echelon is probably the most experienced of the six, and so I will attack him. My wingman can take number two, and hopefully, the other four, possibly inexperienced, will be too confused to retaliate in time to be effective in preventing our initial attack from being successful. Whatever the outcome, in a split second the decision is made: attack the leader, and hope for the best. There was not even one thought devoted to consideration of the intelligent course, which would be to back off and find some easier project. That kind of consideration did not get the 4th Fighter Group to its present stature, and I would not be interested in suggesting that approach.

The adrenaline coursing through the body, at a time like this, denies the existence of fear and focuses all thoughts and actions on the job at hand. Under these circumstances, we are not brave, we are fearless!

Now all concentration is focused on positioning the gunsight on the lead plane. The target grows bigger, the wings begin to fill the sight; hold off a second more, it seems forever, but that first burst of "50s" must do damage to break up the attack on our bombers. The ambushers are about to be ambushed! Now! The 109's wings entirely fill the sight, the controls are coordinated, press the Tit! The Mustang shudders as hundreds of rounds of hot tearing metal are sent crashing on their deadly way.

This morning at five o'clock, I had been awakened by the

subdued swish of the blackout curtains being drawn aside by the "Batman." His gentle efforts allowed a glimpse of a faintly brightening sky, the harbinger of a new day. As I reached for my combat boots, they were gently whisked away to be hurriedly polished and quickly returned before I could be allowed to put them on. This vestige of a far earlier, elitist type of treatment of officers, was due to the fact that this base was an old English base. It had permanent buildings, and more or less family-retainer type personnel in the non-military service functions, such as, housekeeping, food service and valets. These unusual services and surroundings had been maintained and encouraged by the King, who was eager to show his gratitude to those Americans who had joined in the defense of England prior to the entry of the United States into the war.

When the United States had finally entered the fight against the Nazis, the U.S. citizens, who had volunteered and become pilots flying combat missions in the Royal Air Force or the Royal Canadian Air Force, were given the opportunity to join the United States Army Air Corps. There they were assigned to a Group as a cadre around which an Air Corps Fighter Group could be established. This became an experienced and demanding Group, the 4th Fighter Group, which could develop tactics and, in effect, act as a research and training organization while continuing to conduct day-to-day combat operations. Into this Group came spit and polish, newly-trained Fighter Pilots, such as certain of my classmates and I.

We were amazed to see the casual dress of the transferees who had preceded us and were now the more or less permanent base personnel. Hardly any of the pilots wore recognizable U.S. Army-type uniforms. Outside the operational area, the dress included various types and mixtures of pieces of different uniforms which were totally new and strange to us incoming USAAC pilots. They wore such things as bulky sheepskin jackets, huge sheepskin boots, rising to the knees, and blue Officer's caps, with that all important "40 mission crush" worn at a jaunty angle. Embroidered wings emblazoned their right chest, with their wing ends drooping instead of rising, as were the wings of the Army Air Corps types. There was no mistaking the air of self-confidence and *esprit de corps* of these men. One felt immediately at ease flying anywhere, with one of these men leading.

Most of these pilots had flown the famous fighter, the "Spitfire" of the Royal Air Force, in the Eagle Squadrons. When they transferred to the Army Air Corps, they still flew Spitfires but soon were introduced to the P-47. This plane was a U.S. heavy, radial-engined plane, built like a tank. It could and did absorb tremendous damage while maintaining the ability to limp back to base time and time again. The main disadvantage for this Group, however, was its relatively short range. Even with an external belly tank, it could barely penetrate German territory, let alone escort Bombers to Berlin. It therefore became appropriate for the Group to change to the sleek, but more vulnerable Mustang in order to accomplish this sought-after goal.

Five other newly trained pilots and I entered this Group just at the time this transition was taking place. Having had transition training in the Mustang, we were in the enviable position of being some of the relative few who had a flying knowledge of this beautiful fighter-plane. We immediately liked the atmosphere of this Group, the casual approach to off-duty time and the zeal with which these men approached combat. We soon felt at home.

We also loved the marvelous piece of equipment we were assigned to fly, the beautiful Mustang. This kite could take-off from Debden with a full load of ammunition, and with two wing tanks, could fly to Berlin, drop the wing tanks, fight the enemy, escort the bombers over the target, and still return to base with ample fuel reserves. It made sense that the best of Groups should have the best equipment available with which to perform their demanding missions.

Having shaved and dressed, I went to the dining room where we were served a delightful breakfast, by uniformed waitresses. I would have enjoyed an extra cup of coffee; however, not having had the day's mission briefing, I had no idea of my destination for the day, or even whether or not I would be flying. If I were assigned to fly, especially on a long mission, an overload of coffee would require the use of the pilot's relief tube. This is a rather primitive piece of equipment consisting of a funnel attached to a hose leading the liquid out into the slipstream. There it is immediately evaporated in the frigid air or turned into lacy ice crystals such as the substance of contrails. The use of this particular piece of equipment involves considerable technique on the part of the pilot, due to the sitting position and the amount of clothing and equipment restricting him. This is not to mention the double shoulder and seatbelt harness which completely immobilizes the pilot from the knees to the neck. In addition, it is necessary to maintain flight control and position in the formation, at all times, while attempting to complete this complex procedure. It is an operation to be avoided if at all possible.

Having finished my breakfast and noting that it was rapidly approaching seven o'clock, I headed for the briefing room. As I walked through the complex, I could hear the steady drone of the bombers high above, already on their way to a target of which I was unaware. They were grinding slowly upward, joining in formation, encumbered by their seemingly impossible load of bombs, gasoline, ammunition, and crew of ten. Loaded as they were, and with a much lower cruising speed, the bombers had to take-off far in advance of the fighters which were to escort them over the target. In the meantime, for their safety, they would be escorted by various other groups of shorter-range fighters working in complex tandem schedule, so that at no time, while flying over enemy territory, would they be unprotected. As I entered the briefing room, I sensed a tenseness in the air which literally pressed in upon my consciousness. Conversations were subdued, and it seemed that the voices of the participants were slightly higher than usual as the tenseness in the atmosphere tightened their vocal chords. Laughter was subdued and pointless, as if attempting to cover up an unusual concern.

Across the front end of the briefing room, stretched a wide curtain, hiding the secret details of the day's mission. Speculation was that this was to be a big one, a maximum effort. As the pilots took their seats, promptly at seven, the Group Commander entered the room with his entourage. Someone ordered "Attention," and all personnel popped to. At the command "At ease," we were seated and silence was observed, no one wanting to delay for an instant the unveiling of the hidden destination for the day.

Losing no time, the curtain was drawn, revealing the many lines, all of which, in many colors, converge like an arrow, on the big one: "Berlin." The details of the Mission were spelled out, "Take-off time, rendezvous time, weather, anticipated German defensive actions, new flak positions and escort timetable." As the details were spelled out, the pilots made notes on the back of their hands, easily erasable if shot down, so no information would be available to the enemy if captured.

The usual routine continues, such as: pick-up of parachutes, a safety device, but also a reminder of the unfavorable aspect of this occupation, escape kits, and take-off positions. Lastly, the Group leader, the Squadron leaders, and finally the pilots and the alternates are assigned. There are always at least two alternates taking off with each squadron. This assumes that there are enough planes and pilots on flight status to fill the positions. Their purpose is to fill in for anyone who has to abort the mission for mechanical or health concerns. The briefing over, and having been assigned to fly, I head out to pick up my gear and check it over carefully. Finding everything in order, I climb aboard the already overflowing operations truck and soon find myself in front of my plane in the dispersal area. There the crew and crewchief anticipate my arrival and we exchange salutes prior to the pre-flight check.

Our respect for each other is apparent and we share a team spirit based upon our mutual understanding and our operational interdependence. We pilots have a high regard for our crews, on whom our life depends when there is no margin for error, while attacking enemy planes hundreds of miles from our base, over the enemy's homeland. The crews, likewise, want "their" pilot to be the best and to be able to fly on any mission with no mechani-

Roster of 71st Eagle Squadron pilots transferred to the 4th Group-Displayed in 334 Squadron pilot's shack.

334 Squadron had to have its own flag.

One Down, One Dead | 101

Hawker Hurricane flown by 71ˢᵗ Eagle Squadron in the RAF.

Polish Spitfire of the type flown in the Army Air Corps, 4ᵗʰ Group.

335 Squadron P-47 Thunderbolt flown prior to switching to P-51 Mustangs. (Wehrman)

335 Squadron P-51 Mustang. The Mustang is considered by many to be the best "Prop"-fighter plane ever flown in combat.

cal concerns to interfere with his ability to do his best under any circumstances. They share their pilot's victories as if they had actually been in the air with him at the moment of triumph. If he does not return, it is as if they have lost a brother, and there is much soul-searching, concerned with being sure that they have not been a contributing factor in his downfall.

Together, we carefully check the plane and all of its systems. Check and double check, as if it had not already been done time and time again by the crew-chief and his crew as they sweated out the mission briefing and my arrival.

The external inspection finished in good order, I climb up on the wing and settle into the cockpit, where with the help of the crew-chief, I'm strapped into the seat. Seated on the dinghy, with my backpack parachute, the shoulder straps are placed and securely buckled to the lap belt. Being over six feet tall and 200 pounds, I have a tight and not-too-comfortable fit in the cockpit, however, each time I assume that uncomfortable position, I am grateful for my aviation cadet Group Commander's recommendation that I be assigned to fighters. Once I'm strapped in, the helmet is next, with the radio cord plugged into the outlet and the radio operation checked. The goggles are fastened to the helmet for future use and the oxygen mask fastened to the helmet and its operation checked. Next come the gloves and the routine cockpit-check of the instruments. Everything being in order, we're ready to start the engine.

Fuel tank switch on a full tank, prop control full pitch, mixture control full rich, crack the throttle, and we're ready to wind it up. At my signal, "Clear," the crew-chief responds, "Clear," and I hit the starter button. The starter engages, and the prop slowly comes to life, turning sluggishly at first and then picking up speed; the engine coughs, sputters, picks up more speed, and suddenly roars to life with a determined urgency, as if eager to be on with the Mission.

After a short warm-up, the battery dolly cable is removed, the chocks pulled, and the craft slowly turns to face the taxi strip to await my turn in the line of the planes slowly zigzagging towards the take-off runway. On cue, I join the line and begin the zigzag cadence of the aircraft preceding me. It is a strange sight watching a Squadron of Mustangs zigzagging along a taxi strip as if unsure where they want to go. However, the Mustang, being a rear-wheel plane, with a long engine protruding out above and in front of the cockpit, allows no forward vision when on the ground. This necessitates the strange zigzag motion, so the pilot can briefly see the plane ahead and thereby keep from running into it.

Finally, as the planes ahead take-off two by two, it is time to line up on the wing of my section leader, at the end of the runway, and prepare to get airborne. We run up our engines to clear out any carbon buildup from the slow-speed taxiing, check our mags, and after a quick final cockpit check, we push the throttles to the firewall and head down the runway. Immediately, the planes start to roll forward in formation, rapidly picking up speed as the engine roars to full horsepower, and reaching flying speed, they gracefully become airborne. The wheels are retracted and with the lessened drag, they begin to climb rapidly. In the cool morning air, the ride is incredibly smooth. We begin a gentle climbing turn to the left to bring us into formation with the planes which have taken-off before us.

This is accomplished by the lead planes turning and climbing in a huge spiral which allows the following planes, climbing in a tighter spiral, to gradually catch up and, two by two, join the growing formation. Elements join to become Flights of four, which then join other Flights to become Squadrons. These Squadrons then join the other Squadrons to become a Group. Once fully formed, the armada covers hundreds of yards from side to side and is closely followed by the alternates who await the opportunity to join by replacing any plane which may have to abort the Mission. It is most unlikely that all of the planes, originally assigned to the Mission, will be able to continue to the target. Almost always there will be one or two who must abort due to a malfunction, or illness of the pilot.

The Group having accomplished the form-up according to plan, turns east and heads out over the Channel on the way to its objective. The planes continue to climb as they head towards Germany and are abruptly informed of their crossing of the coast of the mainland, by ugly black blasts of flak which always welcome us to the occupied territory of the Nazis. These welcoming blasts are routine, but due to the evasion techniques of the Group, are generally ineffective and rarely inflict any damage. The Group, aware of the anticipated welcome, always engages in evasive action, when approaching the coast. It changes altitudes and direction frequently in order to defeat the German aiming equipment which inevitably tracks any approaching intruders.

As the Group continues uneventfully towards its destination, radio silence is maintained as well as constant vigilance. There will be no surprise attacks on this, the 4th. As we intrude towards the heartland of Germany, we encounter no enemy resistance, and no additional flak is directed at us. Possibly the Germans do not want to give us any clues as to exactly where we are, over the clouds by revealing any large flak-defended area for us to use as a check point.

These are the events leading up to the point at which I find myself boring in on the six 109s with my six 50s spitting their deadly venom.

The Mustang shudders as the recoil interrupts the smooth forward motion of the encounter. The armor-piercing incendiaries blast on their uncompromising way. Instantly, bright, white, flashing explosions of light on the fuselage and wingroots of the Me-109 confirm that the preparations had been correct and the enemy pilot had found himself in an undesirable and untenable position. Suddenly violent evasive action, skidding, turning, and then a desperate split "S," heading straight for the deck, indicates the pilot has finally become aware of a danger which he had not even considered a few seconds before. Directly on his tail and following every move, I persist, firing short bursts whenever I am able to bring my sights to bear.

Fortunately, four of the other five enemy planes decided that discretion was the better part of valor and left for other less dangerous destinations; a quick glance over my shoulder confirms this fact. I continue to follow the 109's maneuvers doggedly, firing short bursts whenever the elusive quarry allows an opening. In a last desperate attempt to escape my vicious attack he rolls into a vertical dive. In the ensuing vertical dive, I have ample proof of the deadliness of my fire. Pieces of the enemy plane, dislodged by bursts of API, (armor-piercing incendiaries), bounce off my plane as I rapidly close the distance between us. This hot pursuit soon becomes cause for alarm, as it appears that I am about to overrun the 109 and myself become the target. At this point, the 109 appears to hit compressibility, since it suddenly starts to shudder violently. In desperation, I dump twenty degrees of flaps. The plane reacts violently to this unheard-of tactic, and I fight the controls to keep the plane on course. Certainly, it is an unusual tactic since flaps are meant to be used to change the airfoil to allow slower speeds for landing and to provide more lift for short-run take-offs. They were never intended for use to lower speeds in situations where the plane is approaching the speed of sound. Amazingly, the design of this super plane is such that the flaps not only hold on, but they begin to slow the descent enough to keep me from experiencing the disastrous effects of passing the 109 and, in turn, becoming the target.

Now suddenly, I am faced with another imminent danger; the ground is approaching at a tremendous speed, and it becomes imperative that I immediately pull out of the dive or end up as a pile of smoldering scrap, boring my way into the hallowed German landscape. Slowly and gently, I pull back on the stick, immediately feeling the effects of the high-speed pullout. My cheeks sag towards my chin, my body becoming heavy beyond belief. Tensing my muscles with all my strength, I suck in my gut until it hurts, straining every facility to keep the blood from draining from my brain, fighting the inevitable numbing blackout that is descending upon me. The world is becoming gray in spite of my best efforts. However, as the air becomes more dense and the plane's direction becomes more parallel to the ground, I gradually ease off the pressure on the stick, and the force of the unnatural gravity diminishes, and the drain of blood from my brain diminishes accordingly. With the "G" forces declining, I find myself hurtling along at treetop level with my sight returning to normal and my senses clearing immeasurably. I dump the flaps and take stock of my situation.

A quick glance over my shoulder confirmed that the 109 had not been so fortunate; there was a telltale ball of flame and smoke rising over the spot where it had augured in. It had been a miracle that the enemy pilot had been able to bail out, his chute floating him gently earthward.

Now barreling along at over 600 miles per hour, bouncing over every slight thermal like a myriad of potholes, it is time to think ahead. A call on the radio receives no response. A second call produces the same result. Alone, unable to contact my Group, and hearing no radio chatter whatsoever, I take stock of the situation. My remaining ammo and fuel would probably not sustain another encounter with enemy planes, and I am a thousand miles from base. My best bet would be to climb back to altitude and head back to base trying to keep out of trouble on the way.

Taking advantage of my extra speed, I gently pull back on the stick and head for the sky. I level off at twenty-five thousand feet and head eastward towards England. Cruising along at 325 miles per hour, I have no emergency with which to contend. For the first time since my encounter, I have a moment to think. Suddenly, I am filled with euphoria as all the pent-up emotions of challenge, danger, combat, and victory suddenly engulf me. The emotional high of this moment exceeds anything I have ever experienced. All my previous training and work has culminated in this, my first aerial victory. This moment I will remember forever.

Flying alone, drunk with the thoughts of this accomplishment, I overtake a plane laboring slowly towards England, at ten o'clock low. I let down cautiously until I am able to identify the plane as a crippled B-17, limping hopefully along, with two engines shot out. In order not to alarm the crew, I slowly edge down and close in to the cripple from the side. As I approach, I flip up my wing occasionally so the crew can clearly identify the angular wing of the P-51 as a friendly aircraft. At no time do I dare point my nose at the B-17 or make any move that could be interpreted as hostile. Any such moves would result in drawing fire from the B-17's fifty-calibers. The bombers are wary of any fighter heading towards them, since it is not unusual for Germans to rehabilitate downed Allied aircraft to test them and to use them to prey upon unsuspecting crippled bombers struggling to return to England.

After making sure that the bomber has had ample opportunity to identify my plane, I climb about two thousand feet above it, into the sun, where I post myself, to be in a position to give maximum support should any enemy fighters attempt to knock down the crippled bomber. In this position I escort the bomber to the Channel coast, and then when it is in the relative safety of the Channel airspace, I waggle my wings and head for the airdrome at Debden.

To arrive alone, and prior to the return of the Group, would be a cause of concern for the crew, so, in spite of a semi-ban on such maneuvers, I perform a victory roll over the field. I come up and around for a perfect combat landing and quickly taxi to the revetment. There, to the glee of the crew, I enthusiastically relate the events of the day and fill in the log and crawl down from the aircraft.

I head to the briefing room for debriefing, which takes place after every mission. S-2 carefully interviews each pilot upon return, in order to obtain any information, however minute, that might be of value in making any future Missions more safe or productive. First, the pilot is given a shot of scotch to help ease off the tensions and make him more amenable to the questioning that follows, and then he fills out his report.

As I was being questioned, the Group started to land and soon the room was full of pilots all talking at once. It had been a successful mission and all the pilots were exuberant, to the extent that it was almost impossible to carry on any conversation. All of us, who had scored, were constantly being slapped on the back and congratulated for our victories. I now felt great relief that I had proven myself. I joined the ranks of Capt. Hively, Lts. Gillette, Lang, Hofer and Fraser, all of whom had scored victories on this Mission.

The debriefing ended, we grabbed some lunch, a little rest, and reported back to the briefing room to be briefed for our second Mission.

This one turned out to be a milk run, a glide-bombing Mission target: Beaumont sur Oise railroad bridge. Two sections, mine included, were to carry two 500-pound bombs each, and the other section was to fly fighter cover.

Our tactic was to position ourselves at approximately 30 to 45 degrees from parallel to the bridge and dive towards it in a 30-degree dive angle. As we dove, we were to fire our 50s, and when they were seen to be hitting the target, we were to release the bombs.

When we dropped the bombs, many hit the target, but I saw mine hit and bounce, and having time-delay fuses, they rose in a graceful arc and landed in what appeared to be a hotel swimming pool, where they unceremoniously detonated, sending great geysers of water skyward. The return trip was uneventful and after debriefing, the pilots headed in various directions in their little groups.

Some who had been in England, with the Eagle Squadrons, and had married English women, headed into town to be with their wives. Others headed for their quarters, and still others headed for the bar. After an excellent dinner, I took in the movie, a new release on the base, well-bracketed with " Fox Movietone News" of Allied successes, as well as how everything was going well on the home front, with the production of planes, tanks, and ships reaching new goals. There were also the inevitable "Shorts" of the men in boot camp and their eagerness to join the fray.

The score for the day had been ten destroyed, one lost.

The next three missions, the 25th, 27th, and 28th, to Chaumont, Karlsruhe, and Ruhland-Dessau, resulted in 12 ½ destroyed with a loss of three more planes and pilots. On the 28th, Mike led his Squadron on an interception of 20-plus Nazis that were about to attack bombers heading for Magdeburg. Mike got an Me-109. He singled out one and fired a couple of ½ second bursts with no hits seen. Suddenly the Hun pulled up and baled out! Mike was disappointed to say the least, he would have been much more satisfied to have fought for his victory. He took a picture of the pilot in his 'chute to confirm his victory and add it to his Squadron's total for the day bringing it to eight, with the loss of two of his pilots (MIA.)

Crews load bombs and ammo prior to take-off on combat missions. (top) Weckbacher (bottom) Ziegler

The 4th Fighter Group Mustangs form-up for take-off on a long combat mission with full wing tanks.

Crews anxiously scan the sky in anticipation of the Group's return from a mission.

A welcome do-nut break.

The Eagles return to roost after another successful mission. (Weckbacher)

Unused ammo is removed and the guns cleaned upon return from a mission.

Some landings were hard. (Both pilots survived, thanks to lap and shoulder restraints.) (top) Lowery (bottom) Boehle

Another wheels up landing. Note the lack of skid marks. When the air-scoop digs in, the stop is almost instantaneous.

New procedures fascinate the crewmen in their ongoing instruction program. (Air Force Museum)

An Airman finds a quiet place for a quick nap. (Weckbacher)

One Down, One Dead | 119

A panoramic view of the Debden Air Base in WWII. The three large camouflaged hangers dominate the view and hide the landing and dispersal areas.

Bottom-Debden Airdrome displays various American and British planes at an open-house for civilians and military personnel.

The GIs and Non-Coms always found time to entertain local children and orphans. (Pool)

Chapter VI

THE LAST MISSION

This particular day was a nothing day. The weather was bad over the continent and showed no signs of improving. Everything was in a holding pattern. As we awaited further instructions, the flight surgeon and I were playing a friendly hand of Cribbage.

After laying down his hand, a particularly good one, he paused a moment, and looking me straight in the eye, he asked, "Frank, why haven't you asked for a leave?" I replied that I was not interested in a leave, I wanted only to complete my tour and go home. He said, "Why don't you take a couple of days and go into London for a little relaxation?" Again I countered that this was of no interest to me; I would like to save my time and spend it at home after completing my tour. "Frank," he said, "I will not allow you to fly another mission until you have taken some time off. You need some 'R and R'; as of now, you are grounded."

I knew that his words were beyond appeal and reluctantly agreed to take as short a leave as was acceptable. Consequently, the next day I was off to Cleethorpes, a town I had visited while stationed at OTU since I had no desire whatsoever to visit London. I had such a passion for flying that taking time off was the farthest thing from my mind. I acceded to his request only because I knew there was no alternative if I wanted to return to flying status.

In Cleethorpes, I went to the YMCA to reserve a room and visited a family I had met casually. They were gracious and invited me to dinner, an invitation which I declined, since I did not want to deprive them of any of their tightly-rationed food. I also had no desire to encourage, by my presence, their teenage daughter, who seemed to develop a severe case of torrid devotion whenever in the presence of a pilot, especially one of American origin. Her adulation was apparent to the point of being embarrassing and extremely uncomfortable. Her appetite was of an intensity that left me with no desire to be left alone with her for even a moment. I had never been and did not want to become a "cradle robber." Accordingly, I took leave, on some pretense, had dinner in a restaurant, followed by a movie, and, after a short and uneventful stop at the "Canteen," it was back to the "Y" for bed.

The next day was spent in exploring the countryside with its many ancient ruins. which have always fascinated me. The history that is still apparent in the English countryside is beyond belief. The beauty and tranquillity belied the fact that there was a serious war in progress.

The following day I boarded a train for the return trip to Debden. Here again, I was fascinated by the English trains. They had quaint little compartments, unlike our large open cars. I also admired the way they were coupled in such a manner that when they started to move, they took off so smoothly that it was unbelievable to anyone used to the clanging, jackrabbit starts of the American railroads. To top it off, they had a pleasant "Toot, toot" whistle which was much more soothing than the whistles I remembered from my boyhood. The pleasant ride to Debden finished, I made a leisurely stop at the local pub. Just to kill time, I played a game of skittles with another pilot, who happened in, and tried to down a mug of "Mild." Since I never could stand the English beer, I'm afraid I left more than I downed. The few English pubs I encountered did not do much for my morale. The habitué's were rather aloof and did nothing to make you feel comfortable. It was almost as if you were to be endured only because of the circumstances of the war. A frequent comment made by British military personnel concerning "Yanks" was, "You're overpaid, oversexed, and over here." I always thought, that we Americans did very little to help change these feelings for the better.

The next day, the 29th of May, once again on flight status, I went through the morning routine and reported to the briefing room as usual. Little did I anticipate what was to follow. Had I had any inkling that I was about to fly my last mission, I would gladly have taken as much leave as they would have given me. However, everything was deceptively routine, and the day's events occurred in their natural pattern.

For some time, not being complete idiots, we had been aware of increased security and had noticed larger than usual amounts of equipment being stockpiled in coastal areas, as well as more and more troops being bivouacked in certain areas. In addition, the Group had been flying more missions than usual, sometimes as many as three a day, weather permitting. Most were short penetration and generally involved strafing and firing on targets of opportunity. All of these circumstances led us to believe that an anticipated invasion was close at hand. Each day we approached briefing expecting that today would be the day. Needless to say, we looked forward to it with a great deal of anticipation.

With these thoughts in mind, we approached this particular briefing, hoping for the good word. When the curtain was down, we looked in disbelief at the many colored lines extending across Europe to a point hundreds of miles beyond any previous destination. Poznan, Poland, was to be our target.

Much to our amazement, the briefing disclosed that the 4th was again to be a pioneer. We were assigned to escort the bombers over the target, Poznan, and then to a rendezvous point north of Poznan, near the North Sea. At that point, another Group would relieve us and pick up the escort duty, allowing us to head back to our base. The theory of this mission was that if we could escort over Poznan and return to England, it would be a snap to escort bombers over any spot in occupied Europe, and then continue on to Russia. This proposed "shuttle" mission would be shorter than the one assigned to us today. This, then, would prove that a shuttle run to Russia was a definite possibility for our escort planes.

It would be an exceptionally long and arduous mission for men cramped in a fighter-plane cockpit without even the Spartan amenities enjoyed by the bomber crews. They at least would be able to walk around and have some hot food and a cup of hot coffee occasionally.

Would I change with them? Not on your life! This mission had all the hall marks of being a good "Show," one with plenty of action. It would be most unlikely that the Germans would let this kind of penetration take place unchallenged. Briefing disclosed that this mission would take-off with the fullest possible load of ammo and gas. The large external wing tanks had already been placed and filled. It would be approximately five hours into the mission before we could depart from the bombers and head for home. The usual equipment, dinghy, parachute, escape kit, and shoulder holstered "45" was issued. Today the instructions were emphasized. Use your 45 only if you are faced with a life and death situation with civilians, should you be forced to land on enemy territory. If you are not in immediate danger, or if confronted by German soldiers, throw it away or surrender it without attempting to use it. Intelligence reports indicated that civilians were becoming very aggressive and severely beating and sometimes killing downed Allied airmen, whereas the German military was still observing the articles of war and was capturing Allied personnel without harming them, as long as they engaged in no hostile action.

The Group took-off as usual with the exception that, with the extra heavy load of ammo and gas, everyone sweated out the necessary longer take-off run. It was made even more uncomfortable due to the presence of an unusually large tree, off the base but in direct line with the take-off run. It was an uncomfortable obstacle on any mission but particularly so today. I found it even more disconcerting since I was not flying my plane, "Turnip Termite," in which I had the utmost confidence. It seems it was due for a routine inspection, which could not be completed in time for this mission. Instead, I was flying the Group Commander's kite, which was practically new and of the latest design. It sported the new "Greenhouse" canopy. What a pleasure it was to be able to see in all directions with no framing to interfere with your view. It also gave the pilot a little more room, and I was pleased to find that I could sit up straight and not slouch as I had to do in the "Termite." This was a good mission to have this plane since it was to be of such an extended duration.

The flight was unusually dull with no action at all for the entire crossing of Germany. Everything went extremely well, in fact; all fourteen of the Squadron planes assigned to fly this mission, made it to the target and there were no aborts. We rendezvoused with the bombers as planned, escorted them over the target, and headed towards the North Sea. Right on schedule the next Group of escort planes arrived and took over. It had not even been necessary to drop our external wing tanks, a prerequisite of any attack. It had, however, been a long five hours strapped in one position, and it was beginning to feel like the common description "Dead-ass" was invented to describe the effects of this mission. I wished any kind of action to take my mind off my aching butt. I didn't have long to wait.

I was flying on "Kid" Hofer's wing, and he seldom let things become too boring. He had more excuses to go hunting and get away with it than any one else in the Group. I always found it a pleasure to be his wingman because he was good, aggressive, and seemed always able to find action. Today was no exception. Shortly, he radioed and said, "I see something I think we should investigate." With that, he rolled over on a wing and headed downward, with me in close formation with him.

Whether or not he had actually seen it, I will never know since I never saw him again, but there off to the South was an enemy airdrome, which I later learned was Mackfitz, with several planes lined-up along one edge of the field. With no hesitation at all, this was Hofer's way and mine as well, we decided to strafe those planes. This was an extremely dangerous undertaking, as airdromes were generally very heavily defended and two planes strafing alone would allow the gunners to concentrate their fire on only two targets.

The normal way to strafe a target such as this is to line-up twenty or thirty planes, line abreast, and cross the field at high speed, on the deck, with everyone shooting at the same time, whether or not everyone had a target in his sight. This maneuver split the enemy fire on to many different targets instead of concentrating on any particular one or two. It also encouraged the gunners to be concerned about firing on their own forces, as the planes swooped across the field three or four feet above the runway. They also had to dodge the fire of six 50-calibre machine guns on each of the attacking planes. It encouraged the "Krauts" to keep their heads down and to remain as inconspicuous as possible.

Nevertheless, there they were, and we came bailing in towards the field at over five-hundred miles per hour right on the deck with all guns blasting as we flew down the line of German bombers. Four planes were blazing as we reached the end of the field, and suddenly I could feel the tell-tale thud of heavy caliber bullets hitting my engine. Almost immediately, as I was turning back towards the field, the engine started to cut out, and nothing I could do seemed able to revive it. I signaled Hofer that I had been hit and was making another pass. As I crossed the field the second time, I hit my third enemy bomber, and my plane started to lose speed rapidly. Since I was now the only target, I was being clobbered heavily and was extremely fortunate to pass the field without suffering personal injury, thanks to the big engine and the rear armorplating. I knew that I had "had" it.

I could not gain enough altitude to bail out, and my hands coaxed every control without avail, so I had no choice but to belly it in. Nothing but woods presented itself, except a tiny clearing close to a village, much too small for a landing, but it was my only hope. How I made it is still a mystery, but made it I did, thanks to the many hours of practicing carrier landings and dead-stick landings. I came in, wheels up, barely missing the trees, and sat it down. The big air scoop provided tremendous braking power and the plane stopped barely inches from the trees on the other end of the clearing.

Suddenly, I became aware of a new crisis pending. People from the village were running towards me, brandishing every kind of weapon conceivable, such as axes, pitchforks and clubs. Their attitude appeared anything but one of welcome, more inclined toward mayhem, and was undoubtedly inspired by the ruckus at the nearby airbase and the visible columns of smoke rising from the burning planes. I decided that I did not want to meet with their welcoming committee and must get the hell out of there as soon as possible, if not sooner.

I quickly radioed that I was down and landed safely and was taking-off on foot. I popped my harness release, pulled off my earphones and oxygen mask and slammed open the canopy. In less time than it takes to tell about it, I was out of that plane, on the ground and running into the woods with a speed I had never attained in basic training. Fortunately, the woods had thick undergrowth and after a short run directly away from the village, I was able to stop long enough to divest myself of the dinghy and parachute, and thus unencumbered, get down to some serious running. Since the undergrowth was thick, I could not see my pursuers, and they likewise could not see me. I took off at a right angle to my original course about a hundred yards until I came to a small stream, which ran across my route. I then ran in this stream, roughly in the direction of the village, until I came to a small opening with a clump of heavy bushes within a hundred yards of the village, which I could clearly see.

Crawling into the bushes, I made myself as comfortable as a hunted person can be and waited all afternoon and evening. The only sounds I could hear were my heart beating loudly in my throat and the distant sounds of the hunters hunting for me in the direction in which they had last seen me. Occasionally a dog barking in the village broke the monotony of an otherwise quiet afternoon.

While I sat there contemplating my options, the Group was heading for Stettin on their way to a return to Debden via a mostly over-water route. After finishing their escort duties, they strafed Dievenaw Seaplane Base where they found 18 seaplanes at anchor. They destroyed two and damaged twelve. Mike contributed to the total by damaging two. The Group total for the day was 14 destroyed with my loss as the only casualty.

At dusk, the frustrated villagers returned to their homes, went about their daily routine, and finally went to bed. After all the lights were out, and all of the dogs seemed to have settled down, I quietly crawled out of the bushes and walked off into the woods, away from the village and the airdrome.

I had the opportunity, while hiding, to take stock of my assets. They were few but of importance. My escape kit contained many items that conceivably could be useful under the proper circumstances. Among them was a folding machete, several fish hooks with appropriate line, and a booklet explaining how to survive in the arctic as well as in the tropics, to name a few. It also explained how to survive in the Channel, if you were fast enough to get into your dinghy before being overcome by exposure. It explained that you had approximately five minutes to complete this operation or else it would be unnecessary to try.

The biggest surprise of the contents was the "escape map." This piece of equipment was customized for the particular mission of the day, everything else being more or less standard equipment for any mission. The escape map was the last thing to be inserted into the kit before each mission. They were beautiful maps, printed on silk, in colors and very precise and detailed. If, for example, your mission would take you to France, your map would cover all of France, Northern Italy and the Pyrenees and the small countries leading into Spain, as well as part of adjacent Spain.

Today's mission should have included a map of Poland, Germany and Denmark, with the North Sea and southern parts of Norway and Sweden. Anticipating this particular map, I was somewhat disconcerted to find a gorgeous map of southern France and the Pyrenees. Having decided that I must rely on dead reckoning and instinct from hereon in, I did my best to remember the geography of this area and came up with a general heading to take me to the North Sea and thence westward and northward to Kiel. From there I would attempt to stow away on an ore-boat to Sweden, where I could conceivably sit out the rest of the war as an internee, rather than a prisoner of war of the Germans.

Having made this decision, I inspected the rest of the contents of the escape kit. Some of the more useful items I found were compasses. Some were unusual, such as one that looked like a button, tiny ones to hide in the lining of your clothes, plus a compass that looked like a compass. There was also a small rubber bag in which to carry water, some crackers and some "D-bar" type chocolate, and a "45" encased in a waterproof rubber container. There were also 45-calibre cartridges containing birdshot, for use if you preferred fowl, rodents, or snake for a meal.

I thought back to my "cadet" training days; nothing had prepared me for this particular type of occurrence, not even the first occasion when I was shot down **OVER FLORIDA!** Yes, I was probably the only fighter pilot ever shot down over Florida. It was of no comfort to me to realize that I was not even one of the enemy, and the pilot that shot me down was a very good friend.

It was a casual mistake, but it could easily have been disastrous. It was the result of poor design and lack of attention to details. I was flying a camera-gunnery mission with my good friend Don Malmsten. We were flying P-51s, in transitional school, and I was to be the target. Accordingly, I was flying "straight and level" while he took a synchronization shot, prior to the start of combat maneuvers. As I flew happily along, my plane started to shudder. My immediate thought was that Don had overrun and hit my tail with his prop. The fact is that Don had pushed the gun-arming switch the wrong way, switching it to "guns and camera" rather than "camera" only. The switch should have had an interlock, but did not, consequently the mistake was easily made. This alone should not have caused a problem had the ammunition compartments been empty, as they should normally have been. Unfortunately, the plane had been on a practice-gunnery mission the day before, and the armament men had neglected to remove the unspent rounds.

So there I sat with 50-calibers flying past, and a few not passing. The one short burst peeled back a section of the wing root and entered the, fortunately, self-sealing gas tank and punctured the propeller blades. This caused severe vibration and forced a very careful, slow RPM landing at our nearby base. Obviously this was not an acceptable approach to training, and disciplinary action swiftly followed. Don got off easily, with confinement to the base, accompanied constantly by a guard, for the short period left prior to embarkation for England. The armament chief was busted from sergeant to private, and life went on, possibly somewhat wiser and more carefully.

Fully provisioned as I now was, I headed off in the general direction of my planned destination. The night was dark, and my fears were imaginable. Even the slightest noise was a cause for concern. I soon came to a country road heading in the general direction I was traveling. Darkness encouraged boldness, and so I followed the road.

Several miles farther on my journey, while walking through a wooded area, I suddenly found myself going through a village, right down the main street. Since everyone was in bed, it appeared not to matter, until some insomniac dog decided to make a federal case of my passage. Fortunately, however, no one seemed to believe this vociferous dog, and not a light was lit, much to my relief. Needless to say, my departure from this village was completed with the utmost haste. The night continued with little victories and little surprises, following one after another. It is really difficult to describe in any comprehensible terms the feelings of a person in these circumstances: alone in a hostile land, hunted, lost, but driven to escape in spite of fear which never rests and having no idea what lies just around the next bend of the road. Frightening is a very inadequate word for this kind of experience.

The night went on and was followed by a slow-breaking dawn. As it became light, it was apparent that I was traveling parallel to a good-sized river. This river was between me and my destination and sooner or later had to be crossed. The river was swift enough that I ruled out an attempt to swim across it, either in daylight or much less at night. The only alternative then was to cross at a bridge. I followed the river, off the road, being extremely careful not to be seen. Eventually, I saw a bridge in the distance. I got as close as I could without being seen and lay in the bushes to watch what was happening. Sure enough, there was a guard at one end of the bridge, who appeared to do nothing but greet anyone crossing the river.

It soon became evident that there was nothing but foot traffic using the bridge. As I lay there thinking about what to do next, two young women came walking up the river, from the other direction, carrying a small hamper and obviously intent on picnicking. Much to my chagrin, they chose a rather hidden spot not more than fifty yards from where I lay hidden in very sparse vegetation. They opened their hamper, from which they produced a bottle of wine, and had a couple of sips. This was followed by some conversation, which I could not hear, but could not have understood were I able to hear it. The next thing I knew they were both stripping down to what nature had given them, a beautiful and ample supply, and laughing and squealing, they jumped into the water for a swim. The water proved too cold for their appetite, and they soon returned to their hamper, from which they produced towels and busied themselves drying each other. One thing led to another, and their naked frivolity, combined with further ingestion of wine, seemed to stimulate their libidos to the extent that they were soon acting out some obviously sexually-orientated fantasies. This was not too difficult to understand, there being no eligible males left at home in Germany, all having been conscripted for military service. I must say that not being a candidate for the priesthood, this was a rather unraveling experience. It was difficult to remember the circumstances of the moment and not attempt to offer my services.

Chapter VII

FOR YOU THE WAR IS OVER

As the afternoon wore on and the air began to chill, the women's libidos also seemed to cool, and they dressed, packed up, and departed. As evening approached, people began moving across the bridge in limited numbers in both directions. Since I could see a church steeple on the other side of the bridge, and from the amount of traffic crossing the bridge, I assumed there must be a village or small town on the other side. Common sense dictated that I wait until it was quite dark before my attempt to cross the bridge. From my vantage point, I was able to see people approaching, heading into town, for some distance prior to their arrival at the crossing. There was only one dim light near a guard who was in charge of security for the bridge. He seemed to let anyone pass who was not carrying an American flag.

After it had become quite dark and the traffic had diminished considerably, I waited until I saw a small group of people coming towards the bridge and managed to fall in behind them and come up quite close to them about the time they started across. One of the people at the head of the group spoke a few friendly words with the guard, and each one in turn just nodded in passing, as did I. In the dim blackout light, I apparently looked no different than the others. The guard went on puffing on his pipe and looked off down the road to see if there were any more coming.

Once across the bridge, I leisurely disassociated myself from the group and angled off to the side of the road to assess the situation. As I suspected, it was a village, a one-streeter, as were many of the rural towns, and it seemed that my most likely path would be right down the dimly-lit main street. I waited until everyone seemed to have left the street and then started through the village. Needless to say, it was a scary operation, because to me it seemed I must look entirely different from everybody else; but my success in crossing the bridge had given me a heightened sense of bravado, and I pushed on down the street.

A dog barked at me, and my heart stopped; I continued on as if nothing had happened. Nothing did happen. What luck! I continued through the town with no further incident and down the road, which seemed to be bordered on both sides by woods. I just kept walking along the dirt road, fearful always, never knowing what I might next encounter. This evasion was turning out to be a very stressful operation.

Continuing on through the night, I passed an occasional house with the inevitable barking dog. I soon became accustomed to them since their masters apparently never paid any attention to them. Other than that, there were no further problems encountered that night. As dawn approached, I could gradually see fields and woods and open farmland. It soon became apparent that the farms and woodlots were in large areas surrounding the farmhouses, most of which were clumped together in small villages This gave me an opportunity to continue to move during the day as well as at night. My plan involved following the road and hiding, if anyone happened along, and passing the villages by skirting through the woods or fields around them. It soon also became necessary to detour around people working in the fields.

Hunger was never a problem; fear or stress, or whatever you might want to name it, apparently took care of this kind of need. It did become a matter of intellect, however, since I knew that I could not survive indefinitely without nourishment. With this in mind, thinking about food became a necessary preoccupation. Should I attempt to steal food? Should I attempt to beg food?

What should I, and what could I do? Each alternative seemed to lead to the same conclusion: I would be exposing myself to suspicion and possible apprehension. As it presently stood, it seemed that no one knew I was around, and I had no desire to give anyone a cause to believe that a stranger was in their midst. Consequently, I decided that until I felt a need for food, I would postpone any foraging attempts.

Shortly thereafter, an opportunity presented itself. Walking along a wood-line, I encountered a farmer planting potatoes. I waited until he was at the other end of the field and hurriedly dug up a couple of the potatoes he had just planted. Back in the woods, I cut off the outer layer to expose the edible portion and ate a couple of them raw. This proved to be a poor decision because within a short period of time, my stomach decided that they were not to its liking and summarily rejected them. At this point, I gave up on this type of option regarding food.

Within a couple of days, I felt that besides food, my body also required rest. Walking possibly twenty or more hours a day, it seemed that sooner or later, I must rest. So I would occasionally attempt to rest in a wooded area where I felt that I would not be subject to apprehension. Each time I attempted to conceal myself and get a little sleep, I discovered that my alertness was beyond my control. I tried to lie down and relax, but the slightest sound, such as the snap of a twig or the rustle of a rodent, would pump adrenaline into my system, and run would become more urgent than rest.

Time began to lose importance and survival became an obsession. I must push on, in spite of lack of sleep and food. Three or four days later, in broad daylight, I was walking down a sandy country road, in the middle of nowhere, through a seemingly endless forest. I was losing my ability to stay alert. Fatigue, lack of food, and general malaise were taking their toll. Suddenly, the world was full of sound. I was surrounded by children who had just been let out of school for recess. They were shouting "Fooseball" and pointing at the partially filled plastic water bag that I had suspended from my belt. Having very few alternatives,

I continued walking and murmured, "Ya, Ya." This seemed to be a suitable response, since they did not follow as I moved away from them. At this point, I was unpleasantly surprised to find myself walking down the main street of a small village with occasional pedestrians coming and going. The "little green apples" which one hears about, now and then, suddenly became a reality in my life. It seemed that recently it was happening all too frequently. But you do what you must, and in this case, it seemed that to continue unhesitatingly would be the best course to take. At least, it would be the most inconspicuous.

Obviously, it was the correct solution, since I walked right through that town, in the middle of the day, with no more reaction than an occasional nod and a smile. To this day, I cannot understand how an unkempt stranger with several days' stubble on his chin, wearing an unrecognizable uniform complete with water bag on his belt, and an American Eagle on his cap, could possibly walk through the middle of a village in broad daylight without arousing suspicion. It was a lesson well learned, however, to be found useful at a later date.

As the days continued one after the other, the mind became less acute. Stamina and determination combined to compensate for the lack of sleep and the lack of food. In a few days, even these could no longer sustain flight, and fear, as a stimulus, seemed to wane. I found myself, one very dark evening, wandering along a trail of loose sand with the smell of salt water in the air. I must have felt my journey was approaching its destination, since, although I was completely exhausted, I felt I must press on. I did just that, and late that night I became completely disorientated and exhausted beyond endurance. I sat down, leaned against a tree to rest, and passed out.

I have no idea how many hours I was unconscious, but when I awoke it was broad daylight. The reason for my awakening was the prodding of my head with the muzzle of a rifle. Upon awakening, I saw in front of me another rifle barrel pointed at my head. On the other end of each of these rifles were German soldiers. There was no room for debate; my spontaneous act as a deaf mute did nothing to convince them of my innocence. I succumbed to their suggestions and slowly stood up, submitted to a search, and joined them for a guided trip back to their base.

Thus began a completely new phase in my career. The trip to their base was uneventful except for the fact that the German soldier leading our procession, pushing his bicycle, was a victim of severe flatulence, apparently a terminal case. I could have sworn that at times, the air could have supported combustion. Tear gas would have been a welcome relief. Much to my chagrin, I was to find, in months to come, just how easy it was to be a victim of the same malady. If nothing else, the soggy, dark German bread had a capability unsurpassed by any food in the world in its ability to sear the nostrils. The Germans had this marvelous source of fuel right under their noses and were too preoccupied with the war to realize it.

A couple of hours later, we arrived at a small German base. A call to their headquarters soon produced a vehicle which, accommodatingly, transported me, under guard, to what appeared to be a naval air station. There I was immediately incarcerated in a small windowless cell. The cell contained a cot. I was given a bowl of what must remain a nameless variety of soup and left to my own devices. Whatever it was, I had never before or since tasted any soup, anywhere, that could compare with the ambrosia which they had given to me. After more than a week without any food, I probably would have felt the same about a piece of sautéed rubber boot. In any event, I savored the soup, crawled into the cot, and was lost to the world.

I had no idea how long it was before they awakened me and took me to what appeared to be the office. There, I was handcuffed to a German soldier and transported to a train station. Then began a trip that I would not want to retrace. We boarded a train and sat in a car full of Germans, both soldiers and civilians. They were replaced time and time again as we stopped at various stations. I seemed always to be a target of nasty conversations between the soldier and the civilians. I did not have to be fluent in German to understand their conversations and gestures. I found myself thankful that I was manacled to a soldier who exuded so much authority. I think that, were it not for his authoritative presence, and the fact that he was armed, vigilante forces would have made short work of me several times during the journey. They became especially threatening during our transit through bomb-damaged Berlin in daylight. The aggressiveness of the civilians was frightening enough, but I also knew that Berlin was being bombed by day and I did not relish the thought of becoming a casualty of "friendly" fire.

Regardless of my fears, which had become a standard feature of my life, we did arrive at an interrogation center, Dulag Luft, with me in one piece and not too much the worse for wear. This statement is based on the fact that there was really no longer much basis for comparison. To be alive and ambulatory is being not too much the worse for wear! Although I previously had no time or desire to be concerned with it, my crash-landing had taken its toll. My back was painful, and now that I was no longer driven, it became a major discomfort, for which there seemed to be no relief. From the same cause, my left knee was badly bruised and did not help matters.

Both of these injuries, which were more of a long-term nature, paled in the short-term when, for the first time in well over a week, I had the courage to take off my shoes and socks. Never in my life had I ever seen a pair of feet that looked more like fresh-ground hamburger. They were one continuous mass of blisters, with blisters on top of blisters. How anyone could continue to push on almost four-hundred miles with these injuries and these blistered feet is a tribute to the marvel of the human body and the chemical forces that help it overcome seemingly insurmountable obstacles, as well as pain that would normally be totally incapacitating.

In due course, I was turned over to the interrogation authorities. It seemed that my troubles would never end. Instead of being on an ore-boat to Sweden, I was about to confront people whose tactics were well known both by rumor and by witness. I did not look forward to this confrontation, but face it I must, with all my remaining fortitude, and hope for the best.

Welcome to Dulag Luft, the German interrogation center, operated especially for downed Allied airmen!

"For you the war is over!"

They unshackled me from the guard, escorted me to a windowless cell containing a cot, gave me a bowl of watery soup and a piece of soggy German bread, and left me alone. As my eyes became accustomed to the dark, I could see dimly from the light entering the cell through cracks around the door. The cell was approximately six feet wide, eight feet long, and about eight feet high. There was a light fixture but no inside switch. Having determined these facts, I set about eating my sumptuous meal. It proved to be about as palatable as it looked. The soup would hardly be found on a gourmet menu, more likely to grace the inside of an old fire extinguisher, while the bread was soggy enough to have been soaked in that same extinguisher. The combination was filling, however, and a welcome break from the starvation diet I had been enduring prior to my capture.

Since there were no scheduled activities, I next explored the cot. This also was missing some of the usually expected amenities. It was a piece of plywood or some similar unforgiving material, covered by a mattress that had long since lost all vestiges of any former resilience. It certainly could not be considered comfortable, but did offer a change from standing or sitting in the dark.

No sooner had I made myself as comfortable as possible than the door opened, and a guard ordered me to come with him. We walked through several corridors and finally arrived at the closed door of what seemed to be an office. The guard knocked and was told to come in, *in English*. We entered a fairly large room which contained a couple of clerical desks, some filing cabinets and a large desk at which was seated a German officer. I would have guessed that he was a Captain, or whatever the German equivalent would have been.

As we approached the desk, he put down his cracker, amply coated with jelly, stood up, stuck out his hand to shake hands, and, in much too perfect English, cordially welcomed me by name. "Lt. Speer," he said, "How are you, will you join me in a snack?"

I declined, to which he responded that there was nothing wrong with having a cracker and some jelly with him. I again said, "No thanks," trying to keep my salivary glands under control. He then sat down and asked, directly, "What are you, with a name like Speer, doing fighting us?" As directed by our protocol, I replied, "Frank Speer, Lieutenant, 0694194." He said that this was not to be a formal interrogation and that I could sit down, and we would just talk without all the military formalities.

Further, seemingly friendly, attempts to get me to talk about my unit met with the same formal reply. He assured me that he only wanted to identify my outfit in order to put me in touch with my friends, so they would know that I was OK. Finally, he appeared to tire of the game and said, "Well, Lt. Speer, you apparently do not want to be sociable, so why don't you go to the clerk over there and fill out your 'Red Cross' form, then we can notify your next of kin that you are safe and in our company"!

I approached the clerk, who handed me a form, with a big Red Cross on it, followed by several questions, in English, with room for answers. He motioned for me to sit down at the empty desk in order to fill out the questionnaire. I sat down and started to answer the questions: *Name*–Frank Speer, *Rank*-Second Lieutenant, *Serial Number*-0694194, *Next of kin*-Marjorie Speer. *Home Address*-604 Chew Street, Allentown, PA,-*Military Unit- Unit Commander,-Target of Your Mission,-Armament,* -Call-Sign etc.

Having filled out, "Name, Rank, Serial Number, Next of Kin, and Home Address," I completed none of the rest of approximately twenty questions, dealing with military information. Thus finished, I handed the form to the clerk with a great deal of trepidation. He perused it, shook his head, and handed it to the interrogator. He glanced at it, scowled, and motioned me to come to his desk. I anticipated that there would be an uncomfortable change in attitude on his part, so I was quite surprised that he continued in his same conciliatory approach. "You have not completed the form; how do you expect us to notify your next of kin?" I replied that there was all the necessary information on the form to achieve that purpose. There followed some small talk, to which I kept responding that I had filled out all the information required by the Geneva Convention, and I did not intend to provide any more. He said "Lt. Speer, since you refuse to fill out the Red Cross form, we cannot notify your next of kin that you are safe and in our company." I replied that, in that case, they would have to go without notification.

He turned to his filing cabinet, from which he extracted a file full of papers. "Lt. Speer," he said, "Obviously, you are afraid to give us any military information, and that is why you will not complete the form. Let me show you why you are being a little foolish." He produced some papers from his file and said, "You are with the 4th Fighter Group, 334th Squadron, stationed at Debden Air Base. You went to Allen High School, in Allentown, Pennsylvania, where you graduated in 1939. You married Marjorie Poust, who also graduated from Allen High School. You entered the Army Air Force and graduated in class 43-I. Overseas you were assigned, as a replacement, to the 4th Fighter Group. The Group is commanded by Col. Blakeslee. The day you were shot down, your call sign was Spider 3, is that not correct?" Since this was the first incorrect statement he made, I readily agreed to it. Looking me straight in the eye, he said, "Lt. Speer, don't fool with me, you know your call sign was Cobweb 3." I knew, of course, that this was true, but did not reply. He continued with his litany of facts, none of which were incorrect, until I felt he knew more about me than I knew about myself.

After some time, he stopped, and asked me if there was anything that I felt I could tell him that he did not already know. I replied that I didn't think there was. He said, "In that case, why don't you fill out the balance of the 'Red Cross' form, and we will then notify your next of kin?" I told him I would not. He said, "Lt. Speer, you know we have ways to make you talk." I agreed but said, "I will resist as long as I am able." Admittedly, I was extremely uncomfortable in extending this challenge but felt I must, even though I could not even imagine what information I might have which could be of value to him.

He scowled, hesitated a moment, then said, "Lt. Speer, you were picked up in civilian clothes; we have only your word for it that you are an American officer. I am going to put you in solitary confinement for a week. At the end of that time, you will be brought back here, and if you still refuse to cooperate with me I have no choice but to have you shot as a spy"! With that, he turned to the guard, gave him an order in German, and I was conducted back to my cell. The door was locked, and I was left alone to contemplate my extremely bleak-looking future.

The days that followed endlessly to form a week, were Hell on Earth. There was no physical violence, no rubber hoses, no threats, no anything. There was nothing but silence and aloneness. Nothing to do but wait and contemplate, "You will be shot as a spy!" A whole week to think about that one phrase. What could I tell them, what could I do? Do I really know anything of value to them? I measured the room, I counted the floor boards, I exercised. I thought, I prayed, I recalled songs. I even tried mathematical formulas. I thought about Marge, I thought about my family, I thought about people.

I wondered how my brother Earl was doing; he also had joined the Army Air Corps. I wondered about my brother Bob, I had heard he was in the CAP or Reserve, I was not sure which. I wondered how my sisters Margie and Marilyn were; I hardly knew them, since I was away so long, and they were so young. I thought about Mom and Pop; trying to run a farm, and Pop working in the steel mill to further the war effort. He had been an Infantryman in WWI, had been gassed and wounded, and was very patriotic.

I recalled Jimmy Keyes, who wanted me to join the Royal Canadian Air Force with him. He joined, I didn't; the penalties were more than I cared to risk since I was contemplating marriage at the time. I didn't want to risk losing my U.S. citizenship.

I wondered how Walt Bachmann, my closest friend, was doing. He had joined the Army Air Corps but somehow was shifted into training as a glider pilot. What a life that must be; every landing is a crash-landing, and the pilot sits in the front! When we had joined up, his father had given each of us a cordial glass of fine French brandy from his most prized bottle. The bottle was re-corked and left to be unused until the two of us could have a drink together after we returned victorious from the war.

Walt and I had been inseparable friends for almost as long as I could remember. We went to school together, and we worked at the Water Wheel Tavern together when we were both too young, legally. We hung around the local airfield, a grass strip with one corrugated metal hangar. We made model airplanes, we memorized characteristics of every plane in each issue of "Janes' Fighting Planes." We saved our money and bought a ride on the first barnstormer plane to arrive at the local airport that would fly passengers for a fee. It was a Ford Trimotor. It was built like a corrugated barn, with no seats, but it flew. It vibrated and shook and bounced, but it was the most exciting thing I had ever done in my life. I knew then that I had to fly, and I wasn't even out of high school.

Not too long after that episode, my family and I moved away. We moved to Allentown. It was only thirty miles, but it seemed light years away. I enrolled in Allen High as a senior, where, being the new kid on the block, I was swept up in the dating game.

I suppose I was handsome, in a rugged sort of way, in spite of a prominent nose. My curly brown hair gave me a boyish look that belied my seventeen years and my maturity resulting from years of a hard-working farm boyhood. A slim waist separated linebacker legs from an upper body full of hard, lean muscles from years of farm work and piling hay bales for a contract bailing rig during the winter months. Raised during the Depression, first son of hand-to-mouth sharecroppers, I grew up with a strict moral code and an overzealous work ethic.

Food on the farms was very basic but plentiful. We had homemade bread and "Johnnycake" from our own wheat and corn, eggs from our chickens, and milk and cheese from our own cows. These were supplemented with our home-grown potatoes and apples, and pork and chicken, fed from the farm produce. Special treats, on occasion, consisted of vegetable soup from garden fare and an infrequently purchased beef knuckle.

Fortunately, I was afforded time to enjoy the pursuit of Scouting which I enjoyed immensely and remembered with great fondness. I learned a lot about ethics, cooperation and survival skills as well as hiking, camping and good fun.

When I entered Allen High School, I never had to ask for a date. What a change that was. Amidst all the dating, there was one girl who was aloof but always seemed to be around. How lucky it was for me.

At first glance, Marge did not come on as a raving beauty with a full dance card. She had stringy, muddy blonde hair and a normal crop of pre-adult skin blemishes. Fortunately, these were destined to be of a temporary nature and were replaced by a smooth, soft, tanned skin that glowed with warmth and desire. Her most lasting traits were a warm and cozy disposition, a real loving person. I couldn't get enough of her. Her physical attributes included a bosom that would make the most nondescript sweater a delight to behold. This was accentuated by a slim waist and narrow hips that had a provocative walking rhythm all their own. Her shapely long legs would do justice to any chorus line. When I finally asked her for a date, she accepted, even though she contended that she hated me. You would be right if you guessed that we ultimately ended up getting married. At nineteen, brains are not necessarily a prerequisite of romance and marriage, but each of us had an adequate supply, enough to know that this was it, in spite of the many competitive influences with our mutual acquaintances.

We seemed to have everything in common: we dated, we sang in the church choir together, we walked, we talked, we shared everything, even on occasion, things that were not normally shared, prior to marriage. When I finally got up enough nerve to ask for her hand, we suffered the ultimate in degradation: both our mothers had to accompany us to the court house to sign for us to get the license, since we were both under age. The neighborhood busybodies immediately concluded that it was bound to be a shotgun marriage. How disappointing it must have been to them when I left for the service a year later, and there was still no tell-tale bulge under her apron.

What a wedding present we received, one month to the day from our wedding day: the Japanese attacked Pearl Harbor. That was all I needed; I had to join up.

I found that rules had been changed and that, even though I was married, I was now eligible for the Army Air Corps. I signed up, passed the exams with flying colors, and was put on the waiting list for a training opening.

Approximately a year later, I was assigned to active duty at San Antonio Aviation Cadet Center. After a gruesome train trip I arrived at Randolph Field, was duly shorn, put into uniform, and started a totally new concept in living.

I loved the activity and the pressure. I pushed myself relentlessly to be the best in my academics as well as in my flight training. The hazing by the upper-classmen was almost enjoyable as I absorbed the information they piled upon me. The flying was a "piece-of-cake" and upon passing my "Primary" flying requirements, my instructor confided in me that he considered me "The Jack Armstrong of the Air Corps."

Back in my dark prison cell, all of these instances seemed light years away. It was as if I had suddenly become an old man, and I was recalling the days of my youth. These thoughts and memories did help me get through that very trying week, a week which seemed would never end. On the other hand, I did not look forward to the end of the week and its most uncomfortable promise. But, end it did. A knock on the door by the guard brought me to reality. He gave me a small package containing some soap, a razor, a toothbrush and toothpaste, and a towel. I was escorted to a bathroom equipped with a shower, no less, and left there. I shaved, the first time in over two weeks, and showered, also the first time in over two weeks, and combed my straggly long hair. I felt like I was again a member of the human race.

Having completed these necessary amenities, I was escorted to the interrogation room to face the inevitable, final confrontation with the interrogator. As before, he was eating crackers and jam, and, as before, he offered me some. Again I refrained, and we got down to the dreaded business of interrogation.

"Lt. Speer," he began, "I reiterate. You were picked up in civilian clothes; (my flight suit had no insignia) you are therefore considered a spy, with the consequences of which we spoke previously." Of course, I did not know at that time, that my week in solitary had given him the opportunity to check into my recent background and determine that I indeed was missing in action and therefore was most likely to be the officer that I said I was. He, however, did not enlighten me to this fact as he pursued the attempt to break down my will to resist.

"Are you now ready to give us the information we want?" I must admit that my reply was rather tremulous. I did not feel much like a hero and was very dubious about my ability to resist, if any of the horrible things we had all heard about the Nazis were to happen to me. However, I mustered up enough courage to reply that, "Name, Rank and Serial Number," was all the information I was prepared to divulge. "Lt. Speer," he said, "I'm sure you know that we have ways to make you talk." Relieved that we were still talking, I replied, "I am aware of that, but I will resist as long as I can." I still had no idea of what I could possibly know that would be of value to them, but our military code had room for no exceptions, and my course was very clear in my mind. After an hour-long pause (which I'm sure was no longer than a few seconds he repeated that I had been picked up in civilian clothes, and, in the absence of any information to the contrary, I was still considered a spy and therefore was facing a firing squad. Under these circumstances, would I not care to reconsider and tell them what they wanted to know? I said, "I am a prisoner of war, and I am not free to give any information except name, rank, and serial number."

There followed another brief, hour-long pause, after which he called the guard and said, "Put him in with the other prisoners and send him to Stalag Luft III." The poker game was over, a game in which I was the only one with no knowledge of the rules and no cards! My relief was almost unbearable!

In due course, I was assigned to an already overcrowded tent with prisoners of all types and descriptions. I was given the standard Red Cross fiberboard suit-case with personal things, such as underwear, socks, toilet articles, and issued a heavy "GI" greatcoat and woolen uniform. There being nothing to do for the next few days, I walked around the camp and talked to other prisoners, looking for anyone I might know. I had many occasions to see what a dangerous occupation I had left in such an unceremonious manner. It was pitiful to see some of the casualties, who had been dumped into the camp, with only the barest of medical attention. There were amputees, with their stumps still swathed in bandages, hobbling around unfamiliarly on new crutches. There were those with flak wounds covered with bandages that had seen more aseptic times. These people obviously lived with pain. Among the hardest to look at were the burn victims, the ones who had encountered the flash fires in their planes without proper cover on their faces or hands.

A pilot flying in combat is supposed to wear gloves. He is also supposed to wear a helmet, goggles, and an oxygen mask. Not only were these items functional, they were protective as well. When flying a plane loaded with 104 octane or higher gasoline, the pilot is subject to the constant threat of volatile fumes entering the cockpit, and any spark can ignite a high temperature flare-up of short but deadly duration. The burn victims were particularly noticeable; wherever there was no protective clothing, there was no skin, just painfully red areas, partially healed and red as a beet. Worse cases had their nostrils burned away, up to where the cartilage began and the area surrounding the eyes and nose horribly burned and fiery red. Still others had their ears missing with only blank red areas left where the ears had formerly been. Others would conceivably never have to shave again or would find it too painful to contemplate for months or even years.

Every day there was an endless line at the dispensary door and every day there were new faces added to the compound. On the positive side, we did receive sufficient food each day and we were dry. The days passed slowly, and finally a group of us were gathered up and shipped out to Stalag Luft III. We eventually arrived and were unloaded outside the fence which was soon mobbed on the inside by "Kriegies," the Americanized version of the German "Kriegesgefangenen" or Prisoners of War. They were looking for friends and starving for news as to how the war was progressing. I immediately saw a couple of friends who reassured me that they knew it would be only a matter of time until I would join them. Everybody needs friends like that! Since I still had my GI watch, they shouted for me to throw it over the fence to them; otherwise, the Germans would confiscate it, as well as any other valuables. Fortunately, I took their advice and was able to retrieve my watch after being "processed" which, apparently, was synonymous with "confiscation" of anything of value. Of course, you were given a receipt for anything of which they relieved you.

Chapter VIII

WELCOME TO STALAG LUFT III

After a warm welcome from friends and the renewal of acquaintances, the next order of business was the assignment of a room and a bunk. As might be expected, I was assigned to a room with a group of total strangers. Obviously, in the close quarters provided, they did not stay strangers for long. After meeting my new roommates, one of them took me on an indoctrination tour of my new home. The camp was flat, several acres in size, totally surrounded by a ten-foot-high, double barbed-wire fence separated by what appeared to be about eight to ten feet of rolled barbed wire. Approximately every hundred yards around the perimeter of the compound, straddling the fence and barbed wire, there was a tall guard tower manned by a German soldier with an automatic weapon and a searchlight. From this vantage point, he was able to survey all the open space between him and the next guard tower on either side of him. Thus, anyone attempting to go through the fence would be caught in the cross-fire of the two adjacent guard towers.

Approximately twenty feet inside the perimeter fence and parallel to it, was a low board rail supported by stakes. This was the guard rail beyond which no one dared step under the threat of being shot by the guards in the nearest guard towers. This impressive security perimeter was broken only by a single gate, which was also manned by armed guards. Through this gate, everyone and everything entering or leaving the camp had to pass, after being subjected to a thorough search. The system appeared to be impregnable to us unarmed prisoners.

Inside this impenetrable perimeter was an orderly array of one-story barrack buildings standing on supports, so that their floors were about four feet above the ground. This served two purposes: one to keep out dampness, the other to allow a special cadre of German soldiers, who were fondly referred to as "Ferrets," to crawl under the barracks and make sure there were no tunneling efforts taking place. They were aided in this effort by long thin metal probes which they could use to detect soft spots in the earth which might indicate tunnel-building activities.

In addition to the barrack buildings, there was a building used for meetings and church services, a cookhouse, and a couple of general-purpose buildings, housing the library and the "Food Acco," the barter exchange. Centrally located was a fire pool and a small parade ground used for the infamous "Appels,"(where all prisoners were daily assembled and counted). At one end of the compound was an open expanse of ground used for recreational purposes. It was the site of serious softball games and even under consideration as a skating rink in the winter— if we could get skates, if we could make a section waterproof, if, if, if, etc. Many projects were long on planning and short on fruition, due primarily to causes beyond our control.

Each barrack contained a small latrine, two or three small rooms for senior officers, and generally about ten large barrack rooms. These rooms could accommodate from ten to fifteen Kriegies (our acronym for the German "Kriegesgefangenen" or war prisoner) each, depending on whether they used double- or triple-deck bunks. In addition, there was a washroom with several spigots dispensing cold water and a so-called kitchen with a couple of nondescript stoves that could, when given enough fuel, (which never occurred) eventually bring food to a state best described as lukewarm. Here the meager meals were prepared as best they could be.

All of this grand resort area had been carved out of an evergreen forest, evidence of which was still visible in the form of stumps and craters, where stumps had previously been dug up and used for fuel by the industrious Kriegies. The forest was still in evidence around three sides of the compound; and the fourth side was bordered by another compound which was separate but appeared, in the distance, to be identical in layout. This, then, was the West Compound; our home away from home.

It was also explained to me that the adjoining compound, was the one from which the famous "Great Escape" had recently taken place. Of the escapees, most had been recaptured, and fifty had been shot (curiously, with none being wounded). Each camp now had an abundance of placards with glaring red borders, indicating that escape was no longer a sport (as if it ever had been) and that for our own "safety" we would best be served by staying in our compound and not attempting to escape. Furthermore, if we should attempt to escape, our German captors could no longer be held responsible for our safety. The placards made a very convincing argument for our being good little "Kriegies" and remaining in camp where we belonged.

In order to help us remain in the compound, as all good POWs should, we were encouraged to attend "Appel" twice a day, first thing in the morning and again in the evening, as well as on surprise occasions, at the will of the Commandant. At these Appels, everyone lined up on the parade ground, by barracks, and was counted and if necessary recounted, in order to establish that everyone was present or accounted for. The count was repeated again in the barracks each night prior to the final lockup. The same routine was repeated every day without fail, regardless of the weather or any other circumstances.

The barracks countdown was particularly interesting since, at a signal, everyone was required to be in his room for the night. At this time the window shutters were closed, regardless of the weather, and the outer doors were locked and barred. In turn, each barrack was entered by two German soldiers who methodically went from room to room and counted the inmates. If the tally agreed, the guards left; and after all had been counted everything was locked up, and the guards and dogs roamed the compound to discourage any thoughts of possible evening sojourns by restless Kriegies.

"Goons," as we fondly called our captors, were the butt of a constant round of extemporaneous baiting, as much as we dared, without exposing ourselves to the possibility of extended, "Cooler Time,"(solitary confinement). As an example, each Red Cross parcel issued to us included a small package of Ascorbic Acid pills, as an aid to preventing scurvy, from our hopelessly inadequate diet. We told the Germans, upon inquiry, that these pills were to make us able to see in the dark. When they became credulous about the veracity of this "fact," we prearranged a demonstration to prove that this was indeed true.

One night, prior to the final countdown, the fifteen of us in our room, having just received Red Cross parcels, set the stage for a grand demonstration. Each of us prior to the lights-out deadline, had arranged some sort of occupation to demonstrate our ability to see in the dark. When the door opened, the guards' flashlights haltingly went from bunk to bunk and to the center table and back again as they saw, to their amazement, Kriegies lying or sitting in their bunks engaged in various sight-demanding tasks, such as reading, sewing, or writing. To top it off, in the middle of the room, seated at the table, were four Kriegies playing bridge, with a hand laid out on the table and a lively game in progress.

The Germans were visibly shaken by this display, and they were muttering to themselves as they progressed down the hall to the next room to be counted. The last thing I heard them say was, "These crazy Americans."

Months later, completely extemporaneously, I provided a break in the monotony with a totally spontaneous interruption of the evening room-count. I occupied the middle bunk adjacent to the door. From this strategic location, I was in the perfect position to cause a major disruption of the normal routine of evening head-count. The usual procedure was for two German guards to enter the room and, each with a flashlight, to proceed around the room counting the inmates, one progressing clockwise, the other counterclockwise. When they arrived at the door, they would compare counts, and if they agreed, they would move on to the next room where they would repeat the process.

The count was normally taken by an orderly and a non-commissioned officer, who of course, was the superior. In the German military, that meant, "Unquestioned Superior." This particular night, as the two proceeded around the room, counting aloud, they approached the door counting in cadence, "Dreizehn, Vierzehn, Funfzehn."(13,14,15.) At this point, in the same monotonous monotone and cadence, I said, "Sechszehn," (16). There was a moment of shocked silence, each thinking that the other had made an error, since there were only fifteen to a room. Immediately, the non-com jumped all over the orderly for having made such a stupid mistake. The orderly, of course, unable to rebut to his "Superior," stood at attention and accepted his remonstrance with no noticeable emotion, even though he was convinced that his superior had been the one who made the mistake.

The non-com then directed that they make a recount. This time the count proceeded as before, with my repeated addition of "Sechzehn," at the critical moment. Again, the poor orderly had to accept an even louder and more insulting dose of abuse from his seemingly demented "Superior." Again the count was repeated; this time, however, the non-com, instead of looking at the prisoners as he counted, was watching the orderly to see where he was screwing up. As they approached the door I felt this game was no longer fun enough to spend "Cooler Time" for it, and so I neglected to add "Sechzehn" to the count.

The poor orderly now endured the most demeaning remonstrance imaginable, standing in a brace, his face livid with rage and indignation, while the non-com vented his fury until he ran out of steam. He repeated over and over that the count was "Funfzehn" and any stupid idiot could have seen that all along. When the fury subsided, there was a moment of deafening silence, and the poor orderly, frustrated beyond human endurance, managed a tooth-gritting, "Ya, Funfzehn." The atmosphere was at the explosion level as the Kriegies held their pent-up outburst of laughter until the door closed behind the departing guards. This proved to be the high point of our usual dull and cheerless Kriegie day.

While still on "Ops" it had been apparent that invasion of the Continent was imminent. Until I arrived in Stalag Luft III, I had no idea that the bloody conflict had already begun on the 6th of June. Since I had been "touring" Germany on foot at the time, I missed the good news. Naturally, during my tour in Dulag Luft, there was no mention by my captors of this event, which definitely would have boosted my morale. However, upon arriving at this Stalag, I was soon informed of the momentous invasion. Bit by bit the news filtered in, both by highly propagandized German radio, and equally propagandized British broadcasts monitored on our clandestine radio. By striking a happy median between the two different sources we managed to keep fairly informed of the progress of the conflict. Basic facts of the war were confirmed with each new arrival in the camp. As additional pilots from our Group arrived, I learned the details of the invasion as it concerned the 4th.

I learned that on the 5th of June, working in strict secrecy, our crews painted wide alternating black and white stripes around the wings and fuselages of all the P-51s. These "invasion stripes" were to adorn all of the Allied fighter planes to identify instantly to ground troops that these were friendly planes and they were not to be shot down. This was necessary because there were to be a lot of low-level support missions flown and the ground forces often would not have much time to identify the speeding low-level planes.

I also learned that on the 6th of June, Captain Mike Sobanski was to lead "Blue Section" on a fighter-bomber mission but had to abort due to mechanical problems. He was then rescheduled to lead "White Section" on the next mission, a patrol to the Dreux area. His #3, Major McPharlin, had to abort with engine troubles. Lt. Steppe, flying my plane "Turnip Termite," then filled the #3 slot. Later, the Section was strafing a train and Mike apparently hit some utility wires. He was heard to radio Lt. Steppe asking him to look over his kite for damage due to the collision with the wires.

They then proceeded to attack another train. Shortly thereafter, Lt. Steppe was heard to say, "Watch those behind you, White Leader." This was in the vicinity where 15 plus E/A had bounced "Blue Section." Nothing further was ever heard from Sobanski or Steppe.

That day I had lost two good friends, Mike Sobanski and the Turnip Termite.

Ironically, the next day, June 7, orders were received at the base promoting Captain Sobanski to Major!

As the summer wore on and fall approached, tensions escalated. There seemed to be no real progress by our Allied Forces. It began to look like we would be prisoners forever. Insignificant little things became the reason for the initiation of altercations, both verbal and physical.

One incident occurred when four Kriegies were playing a card game, using cigarettes for betting stakes. One of the players was becoming visibly more and more irritated as he played and lost several successive hands. Finally, in utter frustration at losing a particular hand, he literally leaped across the table and grabbed his opponent by the throat, his face livid with anger. He commenced to choke the offending player with no regard for the petty circumstances of the moment. Fortunately, the other Kriegies pulled him off before any damage could be done and managed to cool his Irish temper to a state of reason more acceptable to the circumstances.

Another instance occurred when the Red Cross delivered a shipment of boxing gloves. I was sparring with a small but extremely quick friend of Oriental lineage. A tall, large, and lanky bystander, who was a constant source of irritation to his roommates and was always baiting anyone whom he could bully, asked if he could put on the gloves with me. Since we were merely sparring for practice, I consented.

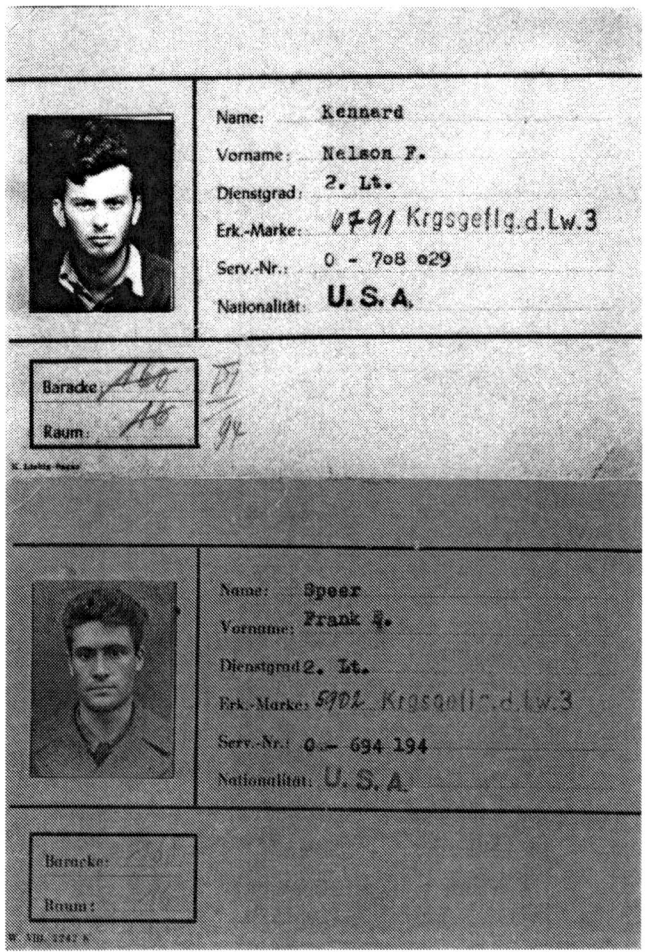

Above–Lt. Nelson Kennard's German mug shot as a POW. It was taken from German files after Germany surrendered and sent to him by a friend. Nelson had been a Celestial Navigator on a B-17 of the 99TH Bomb Group, 348 Squadron. He had been on a pioneering flight of B-17s enroute to Africa via Bermuda and the Azores in May 1944. They were the first B-17s to make the trip without bomb-bay tanks. They reached their destination with little more than fumes left in their gas tanks.
Bottom-Lt. Frank Speer's German ID card sent to him by a friend who had "liberated" it after the German surrender.

Typical entrance to a Stalag with its main guard tower.

The crowded layout of a German Stalag.

A tous les prisonniers de guerre!

S'évader n'est plus un sport!

L'Allemagne a toujours respecté la Convention de la Haye et n'a infligé que des peines disciplinaires aux prisonniers de guerre repris.

L'Allemagne s'en tiendra aussi à l'avenir aux règles du droit international.

L'Angleterre, par contre, a étendu la guerre au delà du combat loyal des soldats du front jusque dans les pays occupés et même jusqu'aux frontières de l'Allemagne, en engageant des détachements de saboteurs et de terroristes. Dans un manuel de service anglais confidentiel tombé dans nos mains

THE HANDBOOK OF MODERN IRREGULAR WARFARE

on peut lire:

« Les temps où nous pouvions appliquer les règles de la compétition sportive sont passés. Maintenant, chaque soldat doit être aussi un gangster et doit — si c'est nécessaire — employer ses méthodes. »

« La zone d'opérations devrait toujours comprendre le pays de l'ennemi, tous les pays occupés et, dans certaines conditions, les pays neutres qu'il peut utiliser comme sources de ravitaillement. »

Ainsi l'Angleterre a commencé la guerre des gangsters!

L'Allemagne protégera son arrière, et tout particulièrement son industrie de guerre et les installations destinées au ravitaillement du front. Il a été créé à cet effet des zones interdites, dites « Todeszonen » (Zones de mort) dans lesquelles toute personne non autorisée est immédiatement abattue. Les prisonniers de guerre évadés, qui pénétreront dans ces zones de mort, y laisseront leur vie. Ils sont donc constamment menacés d'être pris pour des agents et des groupes de terroristes ennemis.

Aussi, nous nous mettons instamment en garde contre de nouvelles tentatives d'évasion!

S'échapper des camps de prisonniers de guerre comporte maintenant un terrible danger. Les chances de s'en tirer avec la vie sauve sont à peu près nulles.

Tous les détachements de police et de garde ont reçu l'ordre strict de faire immédiatement usage de leurs armes contre tout étranger qui se rendrait suspect sous quelque forme que ce soit.

S'évader n'est donc plus un sport!

Red-bordered warning signs in English and French were prominently displayed throughout the POW camps. They suggested that the only safe course was to remain in camp and not attempt to escape.

A room in Stalag Luft III as documented by the author, Lt. and POW, Frank Speer.

A mountain of Red Cross Parcels in a Swiss warehouse destined to feed starving POWs. Each parcel contained the minimum weekly food requirement for one person. The usual distribution by the Germans was approximately 1/5th of a parcel per week, even though the Germans had in storage over one million parcels at the end of the war.

The abominable "sanitary" facilities available for POW use. Many were forty-holers and were heavily utilized by Kriegies ravaged by dysentery.

The gloves on, he commenced to spar with me, showing no intention of causing bodily harm. For a couple of minutes, things went well, but suddenly I received a blow to the side of my head which did not seem too friendly. Oh, well, anyone can make a mistake! The bout continued with me trying to figure out how to get inside his four-inch reach advantage. Suddenly, I was sent reeling with another very strong blow to the head. That was it; that was no mistake. The course was clear, and this was no longer fun. Within seconds, I abandoned any attempt to figure how to get inside his reach. I just barreled in swinging with no regard to niceties. Within short order he was bleeding at the nose, he was reeling backwards, and I was following relentlessly, pounding with everything I could muster. It was fortunate that our fellow Kriegies were available to pull me away, since I planned to give no quarter, and it was totally unnecessary to continue to beat up one of our fellow Kriegies. "Save it for the Germans!" Needless to say, that Kriegie never hassled me again.

One day, shortly after I was introduced to this lovely vacation spa, a new Kriegie, named Nelson Kennard, was assigned to our room. He had been a navigator on a B-17 that had been hit and was burning, forcing him and his crew to bail out over Hungary. When he landed, he was met by an angry mob but was rescued by German soldiers before the civilians were able to do much personal damage to him. Imagine being thankful for becoming a prisoner of the Germans; it probably saved his life.

Nelson was a likable fellow but seemed to me to be in need of assurance, sort of like a younger brother; and we soon developed a brotherly relationship. We became quite close and spent most of our free time together. We saved what little food we could and planned to escape together, since neither of us was willing to accept the thought that we would spend the rest of our days in durance. As time went on we were eventually able to prove that incarceration was not to be a continuing state of being for the two of us.

The food, what little there was, seemed to get progressively worse as time went on. Our mainstay was provided by the Germans and generally consisted of one serving of soup, a couple of potatoes, and two slices of bread per day. Each of these items was of such dismal quality that a complete description of each is in order.

The soups were generally thin, almost tasteless, which was undoubtedly an advantage, and were made from a remarkably diverse and imaginative selection of dehydrated products. None of these was particularly palatable or strayed too far from the vegetable format, and many bore little resemblance to any known vegetable.

One of the common soups was concocted of barley and flour and had a taste and consistency of lumpy wallpaper paste, which it greatly resembled. The undercooked barley, in soggy lumps, hugged the bottom of your cup as if to deny its presence. The glop appeared to have no seasoning whatever, and the serving was small enough not to present a problem in downing it all in one sitting. This particular delicacy was lovingly referred to as *"Gray Death."* When available, we would supplement this concoction with powdered milk and sugar from our Red Cross parcels. It then became what could best be described as minimally palatable. It was always, at best, lukewarm, which contributed very little to its appeal.

To top off this gourmet approach to breakfast, we would wash down the soup with a steaming cup of what we fondly referred to as coffee. Coffee was a delicacy in short supply, it being provided in our always-scarce allotment of Red Cross parcels. Our coffee was prepared in a pot with no strainer and was cooked on our barrack kitchen stove which, short of fuel, struggled desperately to provide more heat than was radiated from the pot in the process. As it was poured, we were careful to keep the grounds from leaving the pot. The grounds were then used again and again and, sometimes, even dried and used still another time. The grounds were reused as many times as possible until we could no longer detect any change of color in the water in which they were cooked. The same process was used for tea, except that generally the tea leaves were dried between each use, due to the tender nature of the product. Both of these beverages were slowly savored, particularly in the winter, when we would wrap our fingers and hands around the cup to warm them, and thus provide the ultimate in energy conservation.

The daily soups were remarkable in their originality. Whatever produce arrived each day became the main ingredient of our "Soup of the Day." As a consequence, we had rare and unusual offerings, such as turnip soup, cabbage soup, potato soup, beet soup, onion soup, and combinations of unknown origin. All seemed to be prepared the same way: boiled in copious amounts of water with no meat stock or flavoring ingredients. The secret recipes were the product of the central cookhouse, where the soups were prepared and where, fortunately, the recipes have since been lost to posterity. Most of the soups had dehydrated vegetables as their base, many of unknown origin. The greenish ones were referred to by the generic name of "*Green Death.*"

From the cookhouse the soup was distributed to the various barracks by Kriegies, who carried large metal buckets full of once-hot soup. The buckets were remarkable in their ability to dissipate heat rapidly during the journey from the cookhouse to the barracks. This enabled us to enjoy our repast in a lukewarm state, with the equation being: the colder the day and the greater the need for hot food, the colder the soup when it arrived. We convinced ourselves, however, that the chill allowed us to much better savor the delicate flavors inherent therein.

The "bread" was truly a remarkable product, the result of great chemical genius. We were to read in a German newspaper later in our stay that German authorities were happy to announce their ability to cut the amount of wood fiber in their bread back to thirty-percent. Even so, the end result was a soggy loaf, with great weight for its size, about the color of a much-used football, and almost as tasty. On our limited diet, this bread in its original state was not digestible without great discomfort from cramps, followed by huge volumes of gas. This created profound distress for our densely-packed roommates. The whole digestive process was finalized by painful and copious diarrhea.

A greatly enhanced degree of digestibility was achieved by placing the slices of bread on top of the hot stove until there was practically no moisture left; thus, incidentally, reducing the size of each slice by about fifty-percent and the weight by about seventy-five percent. The end product was about the consistency of a cinder block, but with the addition of the raw, colorless, German margarine and, on very rare occasions, some Red Cross jam, it became quite digestible and could even be considered tasty.

Next to be considered, on our list of gourmet repasts, was the kohlrabi. This unique vegetable was served frequently, undoubtedly because the stomachs of ruminates could not handle it efficiently. The woody tubers conceivably could be sliced and used in place of parquet flooring. They certainly were not fit for human consumption in the later stages of their growth pattern, at which time they were presented to us. Nevertheless, they were a part of our diet, albeit a very substantial part.

Pea soup should also be given some consideration in this treatise. In this particular case, the peas were very different from any that I had ever encountered. Apparently each pea, at some time in its development, had an egg of some insect laid on it. By the time the pea had reached maturity, the egg of this insect had hatched inside of the pea where it had developed to the point that the insect entirely filled the pea. This alone might not have been too unbearable were it not for the fact that in its growth cycle it had developed a hard shell, which when chewed, had the sound and feel of "Grape Nuts" crunching between the teeth. This insect was probably the major source of protein provided by the diet the Germans, in their benevolence, bestowed upon us.

No discussion of our food supply would be complete without mention of the greatest of all treats, "Blood Sausage." This was the only food source of which we always had a surplus. The ugly brown stuff was totally unfit for human consumption. It definitely was not palatable in its original state. We tried frying it; it immediately turned to runny blood. We tried eating it in its native state; it would not stay down. We tried mixing it with other foods;

it totally corrupted them. The only use which we could conceive was as fertilizer for our abortive gardens, but these were of such poor quality, we were not sure what effect the blood sausage had on them. At best, we found that throwing it out caused the least disruption to our lives.

The one bright spot in our culinary adventures was the Red Cross Parcels. These came from various countries, and each was supposed to contain the minimum dietary needs for one person for one week. Never, except at Christmas, and as we were departing from the camp on our winter evacuation, did I receive more than one-third of a parcel in a week. Most of the time, it was closer to one quarter of a parcel per week, per man. The parcels contained some real delights: Klim (a dried milk powder), canned meats, canned vegetables, sugar, coffee, jam and chocolate. There also were non-edibles such as toilet paper and cigarettes. One of the staples most frequently used was the crackers or biscuits, which were dry and when powdered made a rudimentary flour. This flour was then mixed with dried fruit from the same parcels and appropriate amounts of Klim and water with a little of "Doctor Fierling's Zahnpulver" (German toothpaste consisting primarily of baking soda) to make excellent cakes or "Gedoing."

"Gedoing" was a culinary delight, noted for its sweet and fruity or chocolate flavor, a real break in the monotony of our lackluster diet. It also had the ability to fall heavily to the bottom of the stomach where it seemed to make an audible sound, thus earning it the name of "Gedoing." It was a very heavy and filling dish. It was often judged by our "In-house Gourmets" by such terms as, "it has the weight," or, "just like home." It was considered a delicacy by all, and we looked forward to it with great anticipation. It would always be the "Piéce de résistance" of any special meal.

"Prune Whip" was also one of our original Kriegie delights. It was equally sought after for any "bash." To make it, dried prunes and/or raisins were soaked long enough for them to have reached their saturation point. At this time, they had reached their maximum swelling and taste capability. They then were mixed with Klim, sugar, chocolate, or any other sweet or tasty product on hand. A gentle cooking, if there were sufficient fuel, would then meld the flavors to produce one of the great delicacies of the Kriegie kitchen. As in Gedoing, there were as many variations in the recipes as there were products available with which to produce them. It has been said, "There is no 'bad' Gedoing or Prune Whip."

No bash would be complete without "Kriegie Salmon Loaf." It had "the weight" and was therefore quite filling. Here again, there was great creativity exhibited in the preparation and the list of ingredients used to make this gastronomic delight. Basically, it had some variation of ingredients enhancing the delicate flavor of the canned salmon and "biscuit" flour, such as margarine, salt, pepper, and, if available, cheese. It had even been known to include tomato sauce, although this was not considered a high-priority ingredient.

It may seem strange that we had all these gourmet-type dishes and it may be construed that we ate well as a result. I can assure you, however, that was not the case. I, for example, lost sixty-seven pounds from "fighting weight" in my eleven-month tour of the Stalags. We did, of necessity, eat heavily at times, due to the need to utilize food before it spoiled. Food spoilage would be intolerable, however, and no Kriegie would ever allow it to happen under any circumstances. The necessity for these bashes was the almost criminal way in which the Germans treated our weekly Red Cross food parcel distribution. The parcels were opened and all cans were punctured; then they were given to us. Instead of one parcel per man as intended, we more likely would receive only four or five parcels for fifteen men. The rest accumulated in large warehouses piled to the rafters with the much-needed food parcels. The reason for puncturing the cans was to keep us from hoarding food for an escape; the reason for not distributing the parcels, however, was to remain a mystery.

We had discovered that if we immediately put margarine over the holes in the cans, the shelf life was extended a couple of days with only local spoilage around the hole in the can. This was only a short-term remedy, consequently the food had to be utilized as expeditiously as possible. Since we had no refrigeration to alleviate this condition, our program was based on using all foods on the basis of their shelf life. We ate canned fish products first, then canned meats, then vegetables and so on down the line, saving the least perishable products until last.

In spite of all the Germans' efforts, many of us, who had any idea of escape, managed to put aside some food for any such eventuality. This generally took the form of "Iron Rations." These were a concoction of bits of food items, saved from our parcels, blended into a mixture of high caloric value, and having a relatively long shelf life. As an example, dried prunes were mixed with chocolate, sugar, biscuit flour, nuts, and whatever else of like nature happened to be on hand. This blend was mixed with Klim and enough water to make a heavy dough. The mixture was then baked into a solid block and wrapped in paper to exclude the air. We then hid the completed product wherever we felt it would escape the periodic searches by the Goons.

In spite of the austerity of our food program, somehow we always managed to put aside a small stash of prunes and raisins, which mixed with water and a little sugar, became fermented and provided us with a delightfully intoxicating finale to an occasional very special bash.

Being a military grouping it was necessary to have an organization outside the imposed German organization, which was recognized only out of necessity. The internal organization was set up to provide for functions that were, in our opinion, necessary but not provided or sanctioned by the German organization. Such duties as escape, dissemination of clandestine news (what we considered to be "Sans Propaganda"), and the discovery and disposition of military information were elements of these functions. It was also necessary to maintain communications with our captors as well as carry on all the duties of the day-to-day discipline of a military organization. Senior officers were automatically in charge of these, as well as other duties of command.

The German searches were frequent. They were conducted

The Red Cross Parcel distribution wherein the parcels were opened, holes were punched in the cans and the parcels then distributed.

The twice-daily form-up for Appel. Prisoners were counted by barracks twice daily and then by room each night.

on a surprise basis and were for the purpose of finding any contraband, unusual food supplies, or tunneling activity. On occasion, they even counted the bed boards, which were used to hold up the mattresses and were not meant to shore up tunnels. Each bunk had to have its allotted number, nine boards, or there were explanations in order. Any infractions found, generally called for disciplinary action, which most likely took the form of "Cooler Time." Since this was not one of our favorite pastimes, we became quite creative in finding secure hiding places for our contraband and maintained tight security on our clandestine activities.

Almost everyone was delegated, from time to time, to some sort of duty for the common good. Most responsibilities were on a voluntary basis because most involved risk of one degree or another. Of course, non-voluntary duties of a daily recurring nature were assigned on a mandatory basis. These duties included tasks such as cooking, cleaning, washing dishes, etc., and were not necessarily sought after with a great deal of enthusiasm.

Other tasks included tunneling and related activities, such as dirt dispersal and security, clandestine news-gathering and dissemination, and emergency security and protection preparedness. There were even facilities available for making civilian type clothing and fake passports for anyone the security committee authorized to attempt to escape.

Tunneling and the German counter activities were relatively straightforward and carried on by devious means. In our particular compound, due to the pressure of the recent counter activities following the English mass escape, there were no tunnel construction projects under way (of which I was aware). Due to the tight security of these projects, however, there may well have been activity of which I was unaware during my stay in Stalag Luft III.

News-gathering and dissemination was a well-refined and active preoccupation, which was fraught with serious consequences if discovered, since it was definitely a "Verboten" activity. Heavy Cooler Time sentences would be dispensed, upon apprehension and, of course, there was no court of appeal to which one could turn in case of question about the length of any particular sentence.

The German radio was played over the loudspeaker at the cookhouse most of the day. It was heavy on classic German music and operas. Interspersed, from time to time, was the German version of the War News. This was listened to closely by our German-speaking Kriegie news interpreters and relayed to the rest of us in an open manner, such as by bulletin board. As was to be expected, it was heavily loaded with propaganda. We were able to interpret what was happening to a certain degree by pure logic. For example, if battle lines were fifty kilometers back from the previous day's location, it generally meant that the Germans had retreated fifty kilometers, even though the news may have announced that, "The German Army, supported by aggressive tank attacks and overwhelming airpower, has scored a magnificent victory." We also learned that wording such as, "The gallant men of the Thirty-first Panzer Division distinguished themselves in battle," translated to, "The Thirty-first Panzer Division was wiped out or totally defeated."

The Germans probably believed what they heard, because what they heard was what they *wanted* to believe. It also was the only thing they were legally allowed to hear, there being severe penalties for listening to the BBC for an alternate viewpoint. Of course, the BBC was not averse to a little propagandizing of its own, especially on the news beamed to Germany on a daily basis.

Our most realistic news came through the monitoring of British broadcasts with the aid of a clandestine radio, the location of which was known to a very, very limited number of Kriegies. The news was picked up at predetermined times and was disseminated to a small group of designated Kriegies at a prearranged meeting ostensibly called to study French or some other equally unrelated project. The transfer took place verbally, and notes, if taken, were sketchy and carefully guarded to avoid incrimination if apprehended. This group of runners, of which I was a member, then went to scheduled barracks where interested Kriegies had previously assembled. They were notified of the "Broadcast" by a spoken code word, such as, "Soup's on." The runners verbally related the latest war news, then went on to their next scheduled barrack stop, and repeated the process until all barracks had been informed. This method of broadcasting at least provided the Kriegies with a choice of views, and the various individual interpretations of this news was as diverse and imaginative as were the individuals in the camp. The interpretations were the basis of many vociferous debates and were a prime relief from the daily drudgery of a dull camp existence.

Another very secret task was that of security. A group of physically-fit Kriegies was chosen to protect the Stalag occupants from any unexpected or hostile activities on the part of the Germans or of their fellow Kriegies. Since I was one of the security group, I was quite familiar with their unusual training and preparations.

The main purpose of the group was to provide a defense against any aggressive force that perforce might threaten the Kriegies. The camp was under the jurisdiction of the Luftwaffe, which was considered a weak organization in the eyes of such a formidable organization as the SS. The SS appeared to want to control the administration of the POWs. The recent major escape from the British compound was viewed by rival military commands as further evidence of the ineptness of the administration of POW camps by the Luftwaffe. Since the various German military groups seemed constantly to be attempting to grasp more power for themselves, it was not beyond the realm of reason that the SS, for example, might attempt a coup by surreptitiously taking over the Stalag.

Their well-known methods of "administration" would not be too tolerable to the Kriegies, who were more inclined towards the "Geneva Convention" type of treatment. The in-house security forces were being developed to attempt to help avert any such takeover, even though such attempt might prove suicidal. Another possible scenario might find the Luftwaffe deserting us in the event of a Soviet breakthrough and a subsequent attack by hungry German civilians looking for food supplies. Although they were allies, it was not inconceivable that the Russians might steal our Red Cross parcels in the event they should overrun the Stalag. It also was considered a possibility that internal security could break down and some of our own group could attempt to steal food supplies. In any event, the security force was prepared to take whatever steps were possible to counter any potential problems that might arise. To this end, we were trained in Commando tactics by experienced paratroopers who were, as were we, also guests of the Luftwaffe.

Training consisted of all types of weaponless man-to-man combat, including lethal moves as well as disabling ones. The training was defensive as well as offensive and included methods of killing with your bare hands, or feet, if the necessity arose. A schedule of guard duty was set up to watch over the supply of Red Cross parcels to negate the possibility of pilferage. We also arranged methods of helping wounded or partially disabled Kriegies in the event we were marched out of the Stalag to another location. This, soon was to become an imminent possibility, which was to prove the sagaciousness of our preparations. Our training also included the constant exercise necessary to maintain ourselves in the best physical shape possible under the circumstances.

In addition to the previous activities, there were the more mundane pursuits, such as a multitude of learning possibilities, where Kriegie teachers, some with a little and some with a lot of knowledge, attempted to impart some of it to those of us who were willing subjects. I, for one, at various times, studied French, German, Russian, Philosophy, and Mythology. The courses were hampered by the lack of adequate quarters, textbooks, and knowledgeable teachers. Nevertheless, the classes provided a welcome break from the dull routine and did impart knowledge not otherwise available.

The daily routine went on endlessly; morning Appel, breakfast, lunch, snack, evening Appel, and night lockup and count verification. This was spiced up with the chores of cleaning, cooking, rumor mongering, walking the perimeter, reading, and playing cards.

Those who were talented did many different things to while away the time. There were those who created cartoons of Kriegie life that were every bit as entertaining as anything by Mauldin or Baker, creator of "Sad Sack." Sporadically a newspaper, "The Kriegie Klarion" was published and posted on the bulletin board,where crowds huddled constantly reading all about the "latest" news or rumors.

Imaginative Kriegies created pots, pans, small portable stoves, fans, diaries, and just about any kind of utensil imaginable out of Klim cans. They used only a German-issue table knife, a campstool, and a home-made wooden mallet to fashion these remarkable articles. Wherever there was a need, some creative Kriegie was able to fashion a tool or utensil to solve the problem. One of the more creative crafts I observed was the molding of "clipped wings" to take the place of the "GI"(government issue) wings which denoted the military occupation of the wearer such as pilot, bombardier, navigator or gunner. The artisan gathered the scrapped pieces of food cans which he heated to melt the solder used to hold the tops and bottoms to the sides of the cans. This he collected and poured into a previously designed sand mold of a pilot's wings with one wing clipped. He then placed a safety pin in the molten metal, holding it into place until the metal hardened. Often this arrangement was augmented with a short piece of chain from a dogtag chain, with the other end attached to a small metal ball molded in the same manner. The result, clipped wings with a ball and chain was much in demand and claimed a large price at the "Food Acco," primarily in "D"-bars.

At times, some of the more simple things became obsessions. One such case was one of our roommates who became so vain about the way his hair was cut that only one man in the compound was allowed to cut it. Unfortunately, at one time when he was due for a haircut, the "barber" was too ill to cut his hair. It appeared that it might be a considerable length of time until this could be rectified, and our roommate became despondent and very irritable. I hit upon a plan, and after much discussion and reassurance, I convinced him that my father had been a barber and I, consequently, was quite capable of cutting his hair to his complete satisfaction. I finally got him to sit for his haircut, at which time with much flourish and chatter, I proceeded to absolutely mangle his hair in such a manner that no one could possibly undue the damage unless they gave him a "moony." When he saw the results in the mirror, he was furious, a condition that stayed with him for many days, and I remained as far away from him as possible so as not to invite mayhem. The rest of his roommates were not willing to let him forget his strange haircut, since referring to it always stimulated his primordial passions, and many a good argument ensued as a result.

One of the highlights of our stay in this "resort" was a trip to the showers. It was the only time, in my year of incarceration, when we had the opportunity to take anything but a "whore bath" in very cold water. We marched off to the showers where we duly stripped in the anteroom and went into the already occupied shower room. The room had possibly twenty shower heads around which huddled over one-hundred Kriegies. Amidst all this togetherness we waited our turn.

As we waited, we caught drippings from the showers, which had been turned off, and lathered up as best we could with this limited water supply. The previously showered Kriegies, having dried off, were escorted to the anteroom, and we then positioned ourselves around the shower heads as best we could and awaited our leisurely shower. At a signal, the showers were turned on, and five Kriegies per shower tried to get enough water to wash off all the, by now, dried soap, in the two-minute period the water was allowed to run. It was more than the capabilities of the most resourceful of us could accomplish, so whatever soap was left, had to be wiped off by towel. This shower proved to be one of the most disconcerting events of our stay. Prior to our shower, we were filthy but reasonably comfortable. After the shower, we were cleaner but absolutely miserable for many days. The washing off of the old dead skin and its replacement, with soap residue, left us with unrelievable itching, a constant torment; if offered another shower, I, politely but firmly, would have declined.

Spirits were buoyed by the retreat of the Germans from Stalingrad. They were further lifted by the Allied Forces' breakouts leading to thrusts into Northwestern Germany. Both of these Allied Forces offensives seemed destined to bring the German Forces to an early end of hostilities. Our internal rumor mills worked incessantly. Some Kriegies were packed, ready for repatriation at the drop of a hat. Of course, this was only a dream whose bubble soon burst in a stream of negative news as the Allies were turned back and stalled in the Battle of the Bulge. These were dark days in the Stalag as the Germans appeared to have the ability to again chase our troops off the Continent. "All ist kaput," was an often-repeated comment among the disillusioned Kriegies.

Soon, however, the Russians appeared to regroup and again threatened to overtake the real estate where we hopefully awaited their arrival and our subsequent release. Again the rumors flew, "The Russians were no better than the Nazis and would undoubtedly hold us as bargaining chips to gain concessions from the Allies." "The Russians might well send us to Siberia to man their slave camps." Whatever an active imagination could conceive became a rumor based on "fact." In any event, our security group kept active and in condition for any possible outcome of the events which were taking place from day to day.

Morale of the Kriegies was never lower!

Chapter IX

THE ENDLESS MARCH

Life in camp took on a new intensity. The Security Force was training with renewed vigor. Guarding the Red Cross parcels became a high priority program. The news dissemination took on a very meaningful part of the daily routine. Rumors flew at all times. We lived with constant tension which increased daily. The weather was turning bad and so were our tempers. There was a slight period of relief as Christmas approached. We were issued one Red Cross Christmas parcel per man. The parcels contained delicacies such as plum pudding, turkey, sausages, fruit bars and dates, in addition to the usual items. Soon great preparations were under way for a tremendous "Bash." It seemed that the Germans cooperated by speeding up the delivery of welcome parcels and mail from home. Boxes of "crumbs," once having been Christmas cookies, began making an appearance. We saw more smiles than usual.

On Christmas Day, church services were held and, as was to be expected, attendance was exceptional. Afterwards the great Bash took place following elaborate preparations. We made decorations and succeeded in producing a very festive atmosphere. Menus were printed by hand for the elaborate meals which we had prepared. Our menu consisted of eight courses:

Chicken Soup, Kriegie Salad, Turkey with Gravy, Mashed

Potatoes, Baked Carrots, Plum Pudding, Fruit Cup, Cake, and Coffee.

For a short while, our energies and minds were diverted from the dismal life that had been thrust upon us.

Suddenly it was over, tempers again grew short, and tension increased. Life became even more unbearable. Now everyone was walking the perimeter daily, lap after lap. We were conditioning ourselves for the ever-increasing probability that we would be moved; it seemed unlikely that a move would be accomplished by any means other than by foot.

Then the word came; on January 28, we were given two hours' notice that we were to be ready to depart. Frantic preparations took place. We were issued one Red Cross parcel per man, which we had to carry with us because no one could even guess when our next issue of food would take place. Every imaginable type of pack soon appeared, from elaborate and flimsy to simple and sturdy; these Kriegies had the greatest collective imagination ever assembled in any given area at one time. A great variety of sleds were manufactured as well. Closet doors, bed boards, anything that could be torn loose, became the basis for a sled to haul precious belongings.

Nelson and I settled for a very practical pack design that, in the long run, became more or less a standard, eventually used by most of the marchers. To make the pack, we took a long-sleeve shirt, buttoned it, and fastened the bottom front and tail to the chest part of the shirt. This formed a sort of bag which allowed access through the neck by opening the top couple of buttons. The opening was then covered with a scarf or any cloth available, and the bag became a very practical place to stow and carry any number of items. The cuffs were then tied, by rope, to the bottom of the shirt or to the carrier's belt or together, depending on the taste of the individual manufacturer. Our arms could then be slipped into the loop formed by the sleeves, and the sleeves could be flattened against the shoulders and, assuming the device was packed properly, it became a very comfortable pack. I was very glad for my Boy Scout training when it came to packing and living on the march. I was "prepared" far better than most for the difficult days ahead.

Everyone packed everything that seemed appropriate for a long winter march; food and clothing, of course, having the highest priority. Everything else was left, with the exception of food. Whatever we could not reasonably carry we attempted to eat, some to the point of gluttony. For some, this was to be their last meal. The packs were filled, the sleds were loaded, stomachs were full, and then the snow started; tentatively at first, then increasing in intensity, gradually becoming a fully-fledged blizzard. It even dampened the sound of artillery, which had been heard ever closer and ever louder.

Then it happened. At twelve o'clock midnight, Sunday night, we moved out. A raunchy disheveled-looking group of vagabonds with packs and sleds, wearing every conceivable type of clothing, moved out of the barracks and into the dark and foreboding, snow-filled night. Even the guards and their dogs looked reluctant at the prospect of moving into the unknown that lay ahead.

The motley group assembled in a roughly four-abreast formation extending far beyond the visibility in the dark and bitter cold of the threatening night. Armed guards in their long greatcoats were stationed approximately fifty yards apart along each side of the dismal procession. Each had in tow a snarling guard dog on a short leash that discouraged any ideas a Kriegie might have of stepping out of line. We waited, shivering, while the group was assembled to our captors' specifications and then, at a word, we began to move.

The snow, driven by a fierce wind, stung our faces as we moved out leaving behind the relative warmth and shelter of our garbage-strewn barracks. Now we were facing a world as cruel as we had ever encountered. With everything we owned on our backs, we had not even the remotest idea of where we were going or when we would get there. The outlook was dismal and as time went on, it constantly became worse. We trudged on into the darkness, slipping and sliding on the snow-covered road, mile after mile. We soon learned the routine: march for an hour, then ten minutes' rest, which gave us an opportunity to sit or lie down in the snow and get even wetter and colder than we had been as we walked.

Along about the second stop, those who had packed non-essential items began to discover that they really were superfluous. From there on, the roadside became a great long litter-strewn dump. Everything conceivable, from food to treasured diaries, was tossed by the wayside, as Kriegies found every pound lost became a pound less to torture the shoulders and back. Sleds hastily assembled, with little to hold them together but imagination, began to disintegrate; and as they became impossible to repair, became a part of the litter along the road.

As subsequent rest stops were reached, the constant exposure to the bitter cold and snow began to have cumulative effects on the already exhausted and decimated bodies of the Kriegies. Ankles and knees were most seriously affected from the unsure footing in the increasingly deep and slippery snow and ice. Shoes, ill-fitting or in disrepair, were unable to protect feet from the bitter cold and snow. Soon they were swathed in towels or scarves or anything to help keep the snow out and the heat (what little could be generated) in.

As the march continued, seemingly without end, the Kriegies became more and more exhausted. The ten-minute breaks provided no relief. It became harder and harder to get up at the end of a rest stop. Maybe it was due to the exhaustion and the exposure, but the weather seemed to be getting worse each hour. The wind whistled as it swept ice crystals biting into any exposed flesh. Scarves, towels, underwear, shirts, whatever could be utilized, soon covered the necks, heads, and faces of the shivering Kriegies. It became impossible to recognize anyone.

Fingers and hands, most covered in water-absorbing wool gloves which froze from the zero-degree cold, became extremely painful to most of the hapless men. So the hands too were soon covered with anything available and, as much as possible, were kept in the pockets. This caused even more stumbling as we walked, since we then were unable to use our arms to help balance ourselves as we slipped and slid on the snow and ice. Looking about, I was sharply reminded of pictures I had seen of Washington's winter encampment at Valley Forge. Sometime during this period of anonymity, Nelson and I became separated; I was not to see him again for the balance of the march.

Those of us, on the Security Force, took turns pulling the sleds for incapacitated comrades. As I helped to pull a sled, on my shift, I slipped on the ice and fell on my knees. One began to hurt and became more painful as time wore on. There was little relief when my shift was ended, and the pain continued while walking, even when not helping to pull the sled. I was beginning to feel like I belonged on the sled rather than helping to pull it. More and more Kriegies needed help and sought a ride on the sleds. We who pulled the sleds, in shifts, to help those who were unable to continue, were becoming increasingly tired and unable or unwilling to take our turn at the ropes. My knee now pained at every step and became more and more swollen as time crept unremorsefully on.

Well into the second day, with no rest other than the ten-minute breaks, I began to realize several things. First, we had seen nothing but tiny villages and isolated farmhouses and, with no traffic, it became apparent that we were traveling on little-used roads in sparsely-populated country. Secondly, the German soldiers were not having a picnic, by any stretch of the imagination. Many were older men or men unfit for combat and were finding themselves unfit for this, as well. However, they had a big advantage over us in that they walked in shifts, interspersed with shifts where they rode on horse-drawn wagons. The dogs, as it turned out, were the most ill-prepared of all for the inhospitable environment in which we found ourselves. All had now disappeared. Their feet had developed cracks, and their foot pads split from the cold and ice and were bleeding and sore. Limping painfully, the dogs could no longer continue. We certainly did not miss them.

The march, now probably better described as a faltering, stumbling, slow forward movement, continued interminably. Cold, pain, and hunger were our constant companions. Cramps, diarrhea, and scabies accompanied by mobilized dandruff helped to make life about as miserable as it comes. Added to this was fatigue, mental and physical, to a degree almost impossible to comprehend. Fatigue made every step an automatic, unthinking process, and numbed our minds to all normal functions. We became robots in almost every sense of the word. There were no longer any thought processes. We put one foot painfully in front of the other, endlessly, with no mental involvement. The stinging, wind-driven snow was no longer penetrating our consciousness. The breaks were no longer a respite, just a slight change in pace of an unbearable existence continued by sheer will alone.

The ordeal continued relentlessly. One day, two days, the ranks were thinning. Kriegies were dropping alongside the road, too exhausted to go on, and uncaring of the consequences, just wanting it all to end. What happened to them, we did not know and were too exhausted to even contemplate. Survival was becoming the only instinct left to keep us on the way. Was it survival or sheer fortitude, suggesting that we subconsciously felt that we would not let the bastards beat us, no matter what? I don't know, and doubt that I ever will; but on we trudged.

On the third night, plodding along in the darkness with no discernible mental processes, I felt or somehow became aware of an eerie glow pervading the darkness of the night. It became more and more apparent as we continued on our way but did not really become bright. It pressed in on my consciousness in a manner that made me feel vaguely uneasy and apprehensive, although I can't say I really thought about it. And then I did begin to think about it, and I wondered how an eerie glow could break through my mental repression of pain and cold and cause such unease. It became an obsession: nothing but darkness, silence, cold, pain and this foreboding glow. And then, reaching the top of a rise, before us into the distance, stretched three parallel lines in the sky, glowing green in the pitch-black background. The source of the glow soon became apparent, a very high voltage transmission line, one of which I had heard rumors but had never seen, stretched from horizon to horizon, fading into the snow at either end. The let-down was anti-climactic and served only momentarily to relieve the monotony and pain of our continuing ordeal.

As the long night continued and the now completely automatic footsteps carried us ever onward, there seemed to be no alternative but to capitulate to the weakness of the flesh and not get up from the next rest. My will was weakening inexorably. I did not care what was happening around me; in fact, I did not even know. It was now just me in a harsh and cruel environment; no longer was there any hope of relief. My reserves were drawn down to the point of total exhaustion. I was alone, surrounded by vague forms of others, each of whom was also alone, and each suffering the same endless numbness and exhaustion as myself. We did not talk or communicate in any way, we were all zombies in an alien world, each alone. One foot in front of the other, and again, in front of the other, endlessly. As the hours wore painfully on, each one seeming like at least a day, the agony increased. Some, less able to accept the unbearable pain or mental anguish to the extent that they could not go on, dropped by the wayside. There were no longer Kriegies able or willing to pull sleds. Each one, by now, was reduced to a robot-like status, no longer thinking, no longer a rational human being; we had all become disembodied, with only one function: slowly, methodically, and unthinkingly, placing one foot in front of the other. No longer did we stand or try to be comfortable for our ten-minute breaks. We collapsed where we stood, and only with great effort did we get back on our feet at the end of each break.

We had no idea of how far we had come; mile after mile, as time continued in its inexorable pace. Still no shelter, no hot food or beverage, just shuffling along day and night. For seventy-seven continuous cold, painful, sleepless hours, we stumbled onward with no respite. Many who started were not there to see our destination when we finally arrived. At the end of the seventy-seventh hour, it was becoming light, and we were in a small town with people, just arising, looking out of the windows at this strange invasion. It was bitterly cold, and a freezing wind was adding to our total discomfort. We stood, not knowing the reason for our stop but hoping for a chance for rest and shelter. It seemed like hours that we stood there with nothing happening. I was in a group standing on a stone bridge over a frozen stream, possibly fifty or sixty feet below us. One of the nearby Kriegies muttered, "I've had it," and with that, he jumped over the stone wall of the bridge and crashed headfirst through the ice, and we never saw him again. We did not even know who he was.

As we continued to stand, totally exhausted in mind and body, Kriegies, one by one, started to pass out and drop in their tracks, their bodies completely limp, all desire to live seemingly drained from them. At this point, a German woman, who had been leaning out of a second-story window, yelled something in German to one of the guards. He explained that she said that we could bring some of the injured men up to the second-floor hallway, where they could at least get warm. At that point, a miracle seemed to happen to me; I throbbed to life. I suddenly had superhuman strength; I was no longer tired or in pain. I picked up a man and carried him up the flight of stairs as if he were a baby, and well he might have been; he was crying in pain. I deposited him, leaning him against the wall in a sitting position, and ran down the stairs again and again, each time returning with an unconscious body. With others helping, we soon had the hallway filled with helpless, mindless, blubbering Kriegies. It was far from a pretty sight, frozen feet, frozen fingers and hands, frostbitten faces, but at least now they could be warm.

As I returned down the stairs for the last time, my adrenaline was wearing down, but I was feeling very good. I returned to the street in time to find that other Germans were opening their homes to the Kriegies. I soon found a home with room for one more and sat down on the floor, leaning against the wall, and, warm for the first time in days, dropped into oblivion. Shortly thereafter, we were awakened by a German guard who commanded us to get out, since they had found a place to shelter us. I can imagine the relief of the elderly German couple whose graciousness let us enter their home. They must have been terrified at the result of their kindness. There were unshaven, unkempt Kriegies all over their small apartment. After all, they had been told, in their newspapers and on their radios, that the American Air Force was made up of American gangsters and jailbirds whose sole job was to bomb German women and children. We probably looked the part, huddled against every inch of wall space in their room and, undoubtedly, we looked very menacing to them. I took time to offer our German hosts a can of Red Cross food in gratitude for their helping us. They accepted graciously. Like most civilians, I'm sure they were on short rations and could very well use the extra food.

The guards rousted us out of the house and into the street. The wind seemed even colder and more biting since we had been warm for the first time this winter. As was customary, we stood and waited, long enough to become completely chilled again. When the guards appeared to have their act together, they marched us a short distance to a factory building. We were herded into this unheated building and left to our own devices while the guards set up a perimeter watch.

The building was a large pottery factory with various types of containers sitting around in every available space. In our frustration and possibly to hurt the enemy war effort in any way possible we, with one accord, set about destroying everything that could conceivably help the German military effort. That accomplished, we cleared areas of the resulting junk and gathered the straw used to protect the pottery and made beds wherever we could find a place, ate some of our rations and, promptly went to sleep.

We had no trouble sleeping, our long and grueling march having provided ample reason for a rest of death-like intensity. I believe a cannon could have been fired in the building without disturbing anyone. When we awoke, an unbelievable thing happened. The Germans had somehow been able to manufacture hot soup, and we were treated to a bowl of the first hot food issued since our death march had begun. I cannot remember the origin of the ingredients of that repast, but it had to be the most delicious viand to cross our lips in many a day.

Shortly after having finished our soup, we again were evacuated to the street where we were verbally reprimanded, in no uncertain terms, for having destroyed the contents of the factory. Having thus blown off steam, the Germans again put us on hold until finally they made up their minds to move us further. We were marched to a huge building, which appeared to be an armory or gymnasium or similar one-story edifice. We were herded inside and left to our own devices. Here, however, there was nothing to destroy, so we had nothing to do but await further developments. I spent much of the day searching for Nelson and was greatly relieved to find him well and mobile.

When night arrived, we laid down on the concrete floor to sleep. Now, for the first time since we left Sagan, lying on that concrete floor, I was brought to the realization of the degree to which my back had been injured in my crash landing. There was absolutely no position in which I could lie without pain. Nevertheless, I managed to get some rest, fitful as it was, trying to prepare for the next day's adventure, whatever it might be.

With the dawn came another round of soup and a slice of German bread; our good fortune was unbelievable. Had we realized what was in store for us, I doubt that we could have enjoyed our repast.

It did not take long for us to find out the picnic was over. We again were invited to attend an assembly in the street. We were lined up into our normal marching formation and took-off for parts unknown. At least the weather had moderated to the extent that walking was more comfortable, and we were not fighting cold, wind and snow as we trudged along towards our unknown destination. After a short march, we arrived at a railroad depot. Here we were herded into "forty-and-eight" type boxcars to the bursting point and locked in. Now, in the tight quarters, with standing room only, it was not cold, but heat, and the lack of oxygen, which were fast becoming major problems. The air was swiftly becoming stifling but was fortunately relieved to a certain extent as the train started to move and a small amount of fresh air was forced into the car through cracks in the old boards.

The relief was of short duration since the train's movement was sporadic, coupled with many stops, as switching took place in the yard. It was dark in the locked car, and very little could be seen through the small cracks, but it appeared that the yard had been bombed recently, which would account for the extensive switching. I soon found a weak board in the front of the car, and with the concerted effort of several of us, we broke off a two-foot piece. This did not help us to see; however, it sure provided some much-needed ventilation and was also in a location where the Germans were unlikely to discover it. The improvement in the air supply was unbelievable as the train completed its maneuvers, and we went speeding along the rails toward our destination.

Hours passed with no relief from our confinement. Many of the Kriegies were sick in a way that only someone who has experienced it can fully realize. Horrible stomach pains, vomiting, and diarrhea were disgustingly evident. In order to make things as livable as possible, we soon designated an area in the back of the boxcar for the relief of any of these symptoms. Unfortunately, it was not always possible to make it to the designated spot when suddenly it was necessary to make your way across the crowded car for an overpowering emergency call. It was not long before the stench was unbearable, even to those who might have a strong stomach, and the sickness became almost epidemic.

Hours later, the train ground to a stop, the door was unlocked, and we were allowed to get out for a stretch. The usual complement of armed guards, along with their guard dogs, were in attendance. We were in a marshaling yard next to a town. We could have been in Grand Central Station, it would not have mattered. Seemingly with one accord, we all dropped our pants and relieved ourselves, leaving a horrible mess with reams of toilet paper behind us as we were again herded into the boxcars for the continuation of our journey. This routine became the norm in the days to come. Many a marshaling yard was to receive our trademark in the next couple of days, as we made our way deeper into German territory. Fortunately, we were fed regularly at stops along the way, which helped us to remain somewhat comfortable in spite of the cramped quarters we had to endure.

Sleeping was a necessity but very difficult to accomplish. There were many who were too sick to stand. This made the crowding even worse. We finally arranged to sleep in shifts, with the sleepers along the periphery of the boxcar more or less sitting on their heels and leaning against the walls, while the standers next to them stood close to them and leaned over them with their hands bracing themselves against the wall. This, in effect, gave us a double deck of Kriegies and helped very much to utilize the available space. In this manner, we lived until the end of our journey, the marshaling yards next to our new quarters, Stalag 17D. This, then, was to be our new home.

We disembarked from our vile-smelling boxcars with no regrets; anything would be better than their confinement. As we vacated the boxcar we discovered, to our dismay, that one man did not respond to the order. Sometime during the night, quietly and unnoticed and, unfortunately, unknown to any of us, he had died. The Germans took over, and the rest of us formed up in our, by now, familiar marching formation and were escorted into the vacant camp.

Chapter X

OUR NEW HOME–STALAG 17D

This was a different-looking camp from the one we had vacated. There were slit trenches zigzagging here and there, and there were recently repaired bomb craters in the adjacent marshaling yards. This had all the appearances of being a very lively place. The ground was littered with metal fragments, fallen pieces of flak that had not found their mark. Strewn about were pieces of "Window," the metallic, tinfoil-like pieces of chaff that the bombers dropped from their planes to confuse the German radar. There was trash and filth everywhere.

The same guard rails and guard towers were in evidence. The same low buildings were there, and the same sandy soil was underfoot. When we entered the buildings, however, there was a striking difference. This camp was built for maximum occupancy. Triple-decker bunks were built side by side into racks sleeping up to eighteen people. There were no kitchens; instead there were strategically-placed stoves which served to heat as well as to cook. The tall, inefficient stoves were soon turned on their sides and fire bricks were removed to present more surface for cooking and more heat utilization from our meager fuel supply.

There were no attached latrines, the substitute being strategically-placed latrine buildings. These were marvels of engineering with forty square openings approximately three foot by three foot, side by side in two busy bays of twenty each. The

187

bays were back to back, separated by a four foot board wall. With forty stalls, there was never a waiting line, no matter how many sick Kriegies were in need of accommodations. It was a very public place with a bare minimum of privacy. The system utilized a unique method of sewage disposal, different from any we had ever seen. Unlike Stalag Luft III, where a horse-drawn honeywagon came periodically to pump out the latrines, these spacious aborts were situated over a deep concrete trough in which water was standing to a level approximately five feet below any horizontal surface presented in a squatting position above it. The unusual distance to the water frequently allowed geysers of water to surprise the user with a chilling splash to any horizontally exposed parts hanging over the edge of the opening.

Periodically, a torrent of water was released at one end of the trough, which it rushed through with enough force to remove efficiently the daily deposit of excrement and carry it out through an outlet on the other end. Where it went, no one seemed to know or to care.

The washrooms were in detached buildings, which also were unheated but somehow seemed to be able to withstand the winter weather without, freezing the water or the pipes. It conceivably was due to the fact that the climate was somewhat warmer in this camp, situated as it was, considerably farther south than Stalag Luft III. Needless to say, the water supplied still came in only two temperatures, cold and colder.

Our new quarters were about as filthy as could be imagined. We were told that they had been occupied, prior to our arrival, by Italian Officers. There was credence to this theory, since there were mountains of empty olive oil cans in various locations throughout the camp. We did our best, with very little in the line of supplies, to make the camp habitable. It was hardly a successful venture. We soon found, to our dismay, that we were not the only inhabitants. Lice, fleas, and assorted vermin infested everything, and we had no means to combat them.

I was very fortunate. Although I was an incubator, the vermin did not bother me as they did most people. If they bit me, I was unaware of it. I was, however, apparently a good host and provided a warm, snug site for them to raise their families. Every morning, I could count on looking under my armpits and finding neat little rows of tiny white eggs. Each little egg was securely attached to an individual hair in a very precise and uniform manner. Disgusting as it was, I could not help but admire the beautiful workmanship of these tiny but abhorrent little creatures. Each day the result was the same, in one fell swoop, I wiped out untold generations of the loathsome little insects, and each following day, there was a new generation facing the same inevitable fate.

We now had a new constant in our lives. Prior to this time, we were always hungry and cold. Now, we were always hungry, cold, and lousy. The supply of food did not improve, nor did the supply of fuel for heating and cooking. As a matter of fact, the fuel supply became critical to the extent that we began to take matters into our own hands. We delegated a group of Kriegies to perform a very dangerous mission. Each night, a couple of men would carefully avoid the beams from the constantly moving searchlights and sneak out to the washroom. It was a building sitting by itself in the midst of the barrack buildings, which somewhat hid it from the view of the guards. Its exterior was covered by boards, like all the rest of the buildings in the compound. Feeling that we could brave the wind through the wash-house better than through the barracks, we acted accordingly.

Each night, the designated men, having reached the washroom, would stealthily loosen a board, and, as quietly as possible, pull it from the building. As each nail was coaxed from the framework, the audible creak was muffled as much as possible, and there was always a long period of silence between each succeeding creak in order not to arouse the suspicions of the German guards. The boards were then smuggled into the barrack buildings where other Kriegies broke them into suitable lengths for use in the stove. It was a strange sight each morning to see the wash-house becoming progressively more denuded, until eventually there was nothing but a naked skeleton of framework supporting the roof. It was obvious that the Germans could see this process in action, but they apparently felt no compulsion to attempt to stop the process; at least, they appeared to ignore it completely. Possibly the cooler was full.

We soon discovered that this encampment was not the quiet retreat that Stalag Luft III had been. The days and nights were filled with the sound of sirens, and almost daily the distant sound of gunfire and bombs bursting could be heard. Unfortunately, we soon were made aware of the fact that they were not always to be in the distance. We became awakened to the need for the slit trenches.

One night, while in a sound sleep, I suddenly found myself bodily lifted from the top bunk to crash to the floor amidst a thundering boom. It seems I had missed the siren, signaling an air raid, and a lone British bomber had dropped a twenty-four thousand pound bomb nearby. The concussion of that massive bomb apparently had accomplished this remarkable feat. The rude awakening was followed by plenty of excitement as I dashed hell-bent for the air raid shelter, diving headlong onto the bodies already crouching in the bottom of the trench.

The sky, by now, was full of long fingers of light, slanting in all directions, as the searchlights sought out the precocious intruder. Finally, one having found the bomber, they all converged their blinding light on the hapless plane as if to consume it with one final blast of brilliant light. The anti-aircraft batteries, not to be outdone, sent up a hail of flak as if to prove they could better accomplish the intended destruction. The bomber immediately engaged in evasive action and dropped a deluge of chaff to confuse the aiming radar. The actions were effective, since the bomber disappeared from the circle of light and went on its way seemingly unharmed. Soon the all-clear siren sounded and sent us back to our barracks happy in the thought that another blow had been successfully leveled at our enemy, and the perpetrator had escaped to return another day.

Not too many days later, the Americans gave us a splendid display of daylight precision bombing. They hit the marshaling yards heavily without a single bomb encroaching on the Stalag territory. The raid was accomplished to the sound of thunderous cheers from the Kriegies below, much to the chagrin of the Kraut guards, who obviously did not share our viewpoint of the raid. Unfortunately, one of our bombers was mortally wounded by flak, and the crew was forced to bail out. Imagine the surprise of one of the unfortunate ones whose parachute carried him into our camp, bypassing all the fun of the interrogation center and all the usual preliminaries to becoming a fully-fledged Kriegie in good standing. Sadly enough, he immediately was whisked away by the guards before we could so much as get the latest news of the progress of the war.

It seems that our marshaling yard was an important center of transport for the Germans and may have been the reason for the Stalag being situated where it was. Possibly they had hoped to gain some sort of immunity from bombing because of the proximity of so many Allied POWs. Such obviously was not the case. As if to show the Germans the Allies' capabilities, one night, March 16th, planes came over the area dropping flares. They dumped a precise row of yellow flares followed by red and green flares, outlining our camp. This process was immediately followed by earth-shaking explosions of bombs reaching their targets outside of the camp.

The sky was bright with the flares, the searchlights, the blasts from the bombs, and the subsequent fires. Contributing to the show was the bursting of the anti-aircraft shells, some of which, unfortunately, found their marks and resulted in burning planes slowly descending towards the growing inferno. This fully-fledged air raid resulted in tons of bombs being dropped on the marshaling yards and nearby targets, without so much as a piece of debris falling into our camp. To us, it was a glorious and stimulating sight; to the Germans, it was an onerous act.

We soon learned why our private marshaling yard was attracting so much attention. We learned that General Patton had broken out and was heading across Germany in our general direction, and every strategic supply line for the Nazis was being pounded to deter German resistance to his advance.

It again appeared that we might soon be freed by the Allied forces. Again the Germans decided that we were too valuable to their cause to be left in a position where we might be liberated. The inevitable conclusion was, once again, we must move. And again, we were to provide the means of transport-our feet.

On April 4th, we left our camp at Langwasser and spent our first night on the road at Postbauer. This time the movement was less hurried, more organized, and less grueling. The weather was more moderate, Spring was approaching, and we were not pressed to a forced march tempo. We were covering less distance per day, and each night was spent in rest. The first day out, stopping for one of our hourly rests, I saw dandelions coming through the grass by the roadside. Since I was definitely showing the symptoms of scurvy, I took the opportunity to cut off some dandelion leaves and ate them raw. Having been a farm boy, I was well acquainted with the country practice of spring dandelion salads and the vitamin benefits of this tasty dish. It was not quite the same, without hot bacon dressing, but this did not detract in any way from the health benefits of the product. Nearby Kriegies questioned my activity and were little convinced of the benefits of it as I explained it to them. That was their misfortune, and I continued the practice at every opportunity.

Farther along in our travels, at one of our rest stops, there was a mound of dirt that looked like a storage place for some sort of produce. Digging into it, we uncovered some huge beets, obviously stored for feeding cattle in the nearby pastures. I cut pieces of beet and ate them. I did not again repeat this meal; my stomach was violently upset, and I spent an afternoon ridding myself of all vestiges of anything I had eaten that day.

On the evening of the 5th, the Germans put us in a barn and placed guards around it. The barn had a yard with a high stone fence around it and was adjacent to a farm dwelling. We were able to get fresh water from the well and could move around the enclosed area at will. The Germans provided us with hot soup, and the usual dark, soggy German bread. After eating, we found places in the barn to lay down to sleep. We were crammed in with no room to move around but were at least comfortable on the straw and hay that was in plentiful supply.

In the middle of the night, I was awakened, as usual, by excruciating stomach cramps. I rushed for the door, stumbling over annoyed Kriegies in the dark, and barely made it in time to regurgitate outside the barn. When the cramps subsided, I carefully returned to my niche and fell asleep. This episode taught me to change my routine in the future. From then on, any time we were bivouacked in a confined area, I would place one of my shoes near my head and use it as a temporary depository for anything that chose not to stay down during my nocturnal sessions of cramps. The first thing I did each morning was clean out my shoe and sit it in the sun to dry it as much as possible before putting it on my foot for the purpose for which it was intended. This routine served the purpose and was far less annoying to my fellow Kriegies.

The second night on the road ended in a small town, Berching, with a large central park surrounded by a high black iron fence.

The long, straggling, rag-tag group of Kriegies, exhausted by their long march and decimated by disease and malnutrition, was herded into this park and left to make as comfortable a bivouac as possible, considering there were no facilities available. Meanwhile the armed German guards took up positions around the perimeter of the park on the outside of the fence.

The German grapevine must have worked extremely well, for in no time at all, the park was surrounded by hundreds of curious civilians who had come to gawk at this unkempt assortment of captured enemy terrorists. The German civilians had been informed over and over that the enemy fliers were to be feared and despised for the destruction they had rained down upon their beloved country and for the killing of all the innocent civilians they had bombed. Their propagandists also had maintained that the American fliers had all been recruited from criminal elements wherever they could be found, such as in jails, the Chicago gangster mobs, and other assorted unsavory criminal hangouts.

The propagandists, through the media, referred to us as Luftgangsters, Terrorfliegers, and Bombenterror. It must have been a great disappointment to the Germans to come out to view this terrifying group and instead to find only emaciated, dirty, poorly clothed young men, with no visible ferocity, who seemed as curious about the Germans as the Germans were about them. Both groups may well have learned how it feels to be an inmate of a zoo.

Some, more enterprising than others, came prepared to barter with the Kriegies. Many of the Kriegies, likewise, were of an entrepreneurial mind and, likewise, were prepared to barter for anything that conceivably could help to enrich their lives. The Kriegies were primarily interested in obtaining items for survival or escape, while the Germans were interested in delicacies or pseudo-necessities such as soap, chocolate, American cigarettes, or any other items with which they could enhance their otherwise rather drab existence.

Although most of the Kriegies were looking for food items, such as bread, potatoes, or onions, items most likely to be found in this rural area, there were some who were driven to find more exotic items of which they had been deprived during their long incarceration.

One such Kriegie, Lt. Mike Jacobs, a farm boy from an obscure town in rural Illinois, had been obsessed for months with a craving for a fresh egg and longed desperately for the taste of one of these delicacies. Toward the end of acquiring one of these precious items, should the occasion ever arise, he had, bit by bit, over a considerable length of time, saved one of the most precious commodities available to a Kriegie: cocoa. Cocoa, chocolate, and "D" bars ranked highest in value on the Kriegie exchange. They were closely followed in value by anything sweet, processed meat, including "Spam," which was considered a delicacy, and in descending value, such items as American cigarettes, and lastly, any brand of Continental cigarettes.

Through his frugality and self-sacrifice, Mike had been able to accumulate approximately two-thirds of a tin of the precious commodity and was now prepared to do business. To this end, he toured the perimeter of the park asking in his best Kriegie German, "Habensie ein oeff fur chocolade?" His efforts were soon rewarded by a response from a young woman who furtively gestured for him to come closer. It was, of course, not appropriate to consort with the enemy, and so the clandestine barter was arrived at furtively. It seems she had an egg but was unwilling to part with it for less than a full tin of chocolate. Having finally reached agreement, in the gathering dusk, she departed to fetch the egg while Mike went about the business of acquiring the additional cocoa. The full measure was accomplished by the addition of a small amount of dirty sand, of which the area had an abundance. After mixing the contents of the now-full can into a homogenous mixture, he returned to the agreed-upon meeting place, where he found the young woman waiting with her precious product of the hen.

Both parties being satisfied with the quantity and the quality of the products, the exchange took place, as agreed, and the delighted Kriegie gleefully returned to his friends. After proudly showing off his egg to those in attendance, Mike ceremoniously and very carefully wrapped his new acquisition in yards of toilet paper, one of the few commodities not in short supply, and packed it in the innermost folds of his makeshift pack. There it was to remain safe until a suitable time and place afforded the opportunity to cook and enjoy his newly acquired gourmet delicacy.

Two days later, after many painful miles, the column was bivouacked in an open field near a small wood where there was firewood available for the scrounging. Mike built a little fire, heated his tiny Klim can frying pan, and prepared for the big moment. As a small band of drooling Kriegies watched covetously, he painstakingly, with the touch of a surgeon, slowly unwrapped the egg and with the flair of a master chef, he gently tapped the shell on the edge of his frying pan. A second tap, a little harder, still did not produce the desired result. A third tap, considerably harder, and a final desperation tap, of serious degree, was followed by a close visual examination. This disclosed, to his utter consternation, that the egg he had so painstakingly acquired and so carefully transported, acquired in exchange for his sand-diluted cocoa, was indeed a china egg. Many times, during the remainder of his incarceration, his friends found appropriate occasions to remind Mike of his shrewd bargaining abilities.

Our life continued, drab as it was, with stops in picturesque small towns or barns along the way. The towns had unusual names, such as: Plankstettin, Neustadt, Muhlhausen, Siegensburg, and Oberumelsdorf. One disappointing highlight of the first week's excursion was crossing the Danube near Neustadt. We envisioned the romantic image of the "Beautiful Blue Danube," only to see a very ordinary looking river that looked like any other very ordinary looking river.

Although this march was not at all comparable with the winter march from Sagan, it was miserable in its own right due to the fickle weather. It was normal spring weather with clear days, cold days, and worst of all, wet days. We could well handle the clear and the cold, but wet and cold became miserable, and that state of affairs was not always of such short duration as we continued on our walking tour of Germany. It soon became clear that the length of each day's march was governed primarily by the knowledge of where we could reasonably be bivouacked and kept under guard without causing too much disruption for the local inhabitants. It might be barns, parks, or even, at times, open fields, as the weather became increasingly warmer and less threatening. Along the way, we continually tried to barter with the civilians. Nelson and I bartered with the idea of building up a reserve of suitable food with which to escape. We were really prospering at this time, receiving one-half of a Red Cross parcel every two or three days.

About the fifth or sixth day out, we were marching along in our usual formation, guards and dogs on each side of the long column of Kriegies. As dusk approached, we obviously had not come to our assigned bivouac area. I could see a village in the distance where our column was making a right angle turn to the left. Nelson and I were on the two outside positions of the column. I turned to him and said, "Are you game for an attempt?"

He answered in the affirmative and asked what I had in mind. I said, "When we get to that corner up ahead, where the column is turning left, we will continue straight ahead instead of turning with the group. Don't change your pace, don't look back, don't look right or left; act exactly like we have been told to do this." We arrived at the corner, our hair standing on end. We did not miss a step as we left the column and started up the main street of the town.

How would a rifle bullet feel as it tears into your back, its heat searing your vitals? How does it feel to have a guard dog attack, giving no quarter, as its teeth sink into your leg or arm? We expected the inevitable sound of a rifle or a dog sent to corner us, but not even a "Halt" was heard. True to our plan, we did not look back, but continued to "nonchalantly" saunter up the main street of that town, smiling at the civilians we encountered as we climbed the hill and found ourselves out of town and in the country again. It was just unbelievable that two POWs could leave a column, closely guarded by armed guards and dogs, and walk off into the sunset, past the local inhabitants, meanwhile dressed in American Air Force uniforms, with Air Force insignia on our shoulders, and no one even questioned our actions.

We continued along the country road as it became darker and soon became pitch black. It was difficult staying on the road in the darkness, and as we thought of holing up for the night, we saw lights approaching from both the front and the back of us. We decided the time was now and left the road, climbing up the bank, where we continued to walk a short distance to escape detection. We had not gone fifty feet when we had the terrifying experience of running out of earth under our feet. Suddenly, we were in space, then tumbling down a very steep embankment, terrified at not knowing what would be our fate. Our packs were torn off as we descended, and we were bruised and scarred. Then our descent was slowed by a lessening of the angle of the slope before we eventually stopped rolling and ended up on a fairly even footing again. We stayed there until morning, hardly daring to move, not knowing what our situation was.

As it became light, we were able to see that we had fallen off a small cliff and had ended up on fairly level ground at the bottom. We were bruised and sore but not seriously hurt. Our packs with our escape supplies had been torn off in the fall and were presumably scattered over the mountainside. At least, we were unable to find anything of value. A study of the area indicated that it was too wild and unpredictable to attempt to move at night. With no supplies and absolutely no idea of where we were, it seemed like a very poor opportunity to attempt to escape. Nelson and I both agreed that our best bet was to allow ourselves to be recaptured and go with the flow until a more favorable opportunity for escape presented itself.

Recapture was almost as easy as was our temporary escape. We soon were back in the column again and living the easy life of a Kriegie intent on seeing Germany on foot. Nothing exciting happened for the next few days with the exception of one incident. We were traveling along the road, which had been built up across a valley between two hills, when suddenly two P-51s appeared, heading toward us at combat speed. In less time than it takes to tell, all of us with one accord, were diving off the road and down the banks as fast as we could go. The planes buzzed us at an altitude of less than fifty feet, waggled their wings in recognition, and took off for other parts at a high rate of speed. It was a most welcome sight, but we would have appreciated a little warning.

After a couple of uneventful days, we arrived at a large open field of pasture-land, near Oberemsdorf, where we were to spend four nights. We were bivouacked there and left more or less to our own devices, with the usual perimeter guard in attendance. We had a bonanza distribution of Red Cross parcels. We each received 1/4 of an American, 1/4 of an English, and 1/4 of a Belgian parcel per person during our stay here. The parcel distribution gave Nelson and me an opportunity to gather some seed rations, and we developed a plan to enhance our escape possibilities.

A careful assessment of our campsite indicated a weak link

in the security system. At the high end of the field, there was a shallow ravine leading up the hill toward a wood. There was a guard posted nearby, but he most likely was prone to nap since there was no real excitement, and it was unlikely that he would be able to see movement in the dusk even if he were alert. Our plan then developed to move, just before dawn, up the ravine on our stomachs, into the woods and then over the hill. We felt there must be a small village over there, having seen chimney smoke the day before. On schedule, we moved out in the darkest part of the night, just before dawn, and the plan worked perfectly. As anticipated, we arrived at a small hill overlooking a little village of farmhouses. The farmhouses were separated nicely, so it would be easy to visit one on the outskirts without being seen from the others.

Accordingly, we went down the hill and approached the end house and knocked on the door. A chunky woman came to the door. She did not seem to be the least bit upset at our appearance. In our best "Pidgin German" we asked, "Habenzie brot fur Saifa," The answer was "Ya," and we soon traded a bar of soap for a loaf of the best German bread we had ever seen. This was none of your production, thirty percent wood fiber, soggy, dark bread. This was white bread with a perfectly browned, crisp crust that was crying out to be eaten on the spot. We shoved it into a pack to take away the temptation, thanked her, and moved across the street for another attempt. Again we were successful, picking up some onions and a couple of eggs. In order not to wear out our welcome, we headed back up the hill and into the wood. There we waited for dusk to cross back into the camp. We feasted on beautiful, crispy white bread and Red Cross coffee, and with full stomachs, rolled up in our blankets and slept like babies.

In order to build up our supplies for escape, we planned to take another foray the following morning. We successfully repeated our maneuver, with no hitches, and, in order not to establish a pattern, we went to the other end of the village for our barter operation. We again were successful and again re-entered the camp undetected. Everything was going too well. As if to prove it, one of the Kriegies who was sleeping near us, approached and asked how we were able to live so well when no one else had the kind of food we had. After explaining our operation, he more or less blackmailed us into taking him with us on the next excursion.

    The next morning, as usual, we took off through the ravine. Nothing unusual seemed to be happening, and so we entered the village and started to knock on doors. Nelson and our "guest" were on one side of the street, and I was on the other. As I left the first house, I looked up the street to the other end of the village and saw two figures in the unmistakable black uniform of the SS. I called across the street to my companions, and we headed back towards the camp. At this time, the SS men started to move in on us, shooting as they came. They were firing rifles, not automatic weapons, and were unable to hit the broad side of a barn door, from their one hundred yard distance, let alone a couple of Kriegies in full flight. As we ran, we headed away from them and turned left into the wood towards camp. After running about fifty yards, we again turned left, back towards the village, up the hill, through the wood, to the edge where we sat the rest of the day, overlooking the village and the street. We watched as the SS and their troops searched for us in the direction in which we had headed, towards the camp where they expected us to have gone. The Kraut mind apparently could not conceive of any action except the obvious. That's what we counted on.

    After a couple of hours, they gave up their search and returned to the village. The thought of their presence altered any plans we may have had regarding any future food forays. As dusk approached, we headed back to camp, crawled carefully through the ravine, and bedded down for the night. The next morning, our new found companion let it be known that he was no longer envious of our lifestyle and would not care to accompany us on any future excursions under any circumstances. We were not at all upset by his decision. As it turned out, there were no decisions to be made, since the Germans had us assemble and moved us on towards our next destination.

It soon became apparent, when we were confined to a barn for the night, that each morning the guards would rout us out of the barn and then return and search for stragglers. It was obvious that they had no idea how many POWs had been occupying the barn because they would then plunge bayonets into the hay or straw to make certain no one had been left behind. An idea for escape began to form in my mind.

The rugged hills soon disappeared and we were now in gently rolling country, with farm fields and scattered woods. This looked more like escape country and we had full knapsacks. That night, we were quartered in an isolated barn, adjacent to a farmhouse, along the road. Nelson and I agreed that this was it. We grabbed positions along the wall in the haymow. We spent a couple of hours digging down into the hay, below bayonet level. We were fortunate that the outer walls were of old wood with large cracks between them, which gave us plenty of air as well as a limited view of the area. We crawled into our sanctuary and slept.

In the morning, the Krauts rousted out the Kriegies into the dreary rainy Spring day. They received their ration of soup and soggy bread and then were started down the road in a continuing southerly direction. When it appeared that all of the Kriegies were on their way, we uncovered ourselves and descended from the haymow. It being a rainy day, the farmer was grinding grain, using a noisy gas engine, and so it was easy to depart undetected. We went down the road, heading south, feeling miserable in the rain. We kept a constant lookout for others on the road, not wanting to prematurely end our bid for freedom.

A couple of hours later, I caught sight of two figures following us at quite a distance. Since we were adjacent to a woods, we went into the wood and sought cover in order to let these people pass. As they came abreast of our hiding place, they were engaged in animated conversation. I became aware that they were speaking in French, not German. Having studied French in school, I accosted them and asked if they could help us. They explained that they were forced laborers, free to work on the farms during the day and then locked up at night. They told us to continue to hide where we were, and they would return at dusk to pick us up.

We waited, not knowing whether or not to believe them, but having few other options. They did return and led us to their compound in a tiny village with the unlikely name of Dumseilboldsdorf, approximately five kilometers north of Mooseburg, which we understood to be our destination. It was the second floor of a farm outbuilding and housed eight prisoners. There were eight individual bunks around the wall, each with a mammoth feather tick, there was a table where they ate, and a few chairs. They told us that the village master came each night to lock them up and that when he came, we would be hidden under the huge feather ticks. He came, he talked and joked with the Frenchmen, locked the door, and left. Within ten minutes, there was a knock on the door, two soldiers entered, and we were promptly escorted out of the building and turned over to the nearest contingent of marching Kriegies.

That night we repeated our "burrow in the hay" routine and wasted no time in returning to our French "Friends." This time I made it clear that anyone who might be tempted to betray us would find himself dead in the morning, at my hands. I could not understand French, spoken rapidly, but had the distinct feeling that my position was rather strongly reinforced by the French contingent that did not believe in aiding and abetting the Boche. The end result was that we slept well and received no more visits from the Krauts.

Chapter XI

C'EST FINI

The next morning the Frenchmen were awakened on cue, had their breakfast, in which Nelson and I joined, and took off for the fields. We stayed in the building most of the day, watching the comings and goings of the natives, of which there were few. We thought it imprudent to venture outside, since we would feel conspicuous even though no one else felt that we were. At lunch time, a couple of the Frenchmen appeared with food for us and departed again after reassuring us that all was well. That evening, the Frenchmen returned from their labors loaded down with, to us, exotic foods they had stolen for us. They brought delicious white bread, fresh milk, and a splendid treat, bacon, among other things. We were overwhelmed with the ensuing feast, the likes of which we had not seen in almost a year. We went to bed with full stomachs.

The days that followed, were all similar in pattern with the exception that soon, on occasion, we began to venture outside. Eventually, as we became braver, we spent more and more time outside. The Frenchmen were good providers and kept us well supplied with stolen foods; where they found them, we never knew nor did we attempt to find out. I guess we were just as happy not knowing, as we continued to live, "High on the Hog."

At night, when they returned for lock-up, the evenings became social events as more and more we were accepted into their confidence. We had discussions, though limited by our language barriers. We even got involved in bridge games, due to the relative ease of learning the few words necessary to bid. We did have some interesting evenings.

One noon, as if to punctuate the monotony of our existence, Jean, who seemed to be the leader of the group, appeared unannounced and told us he was taking us to the local tavern for lunch. Our many protestations were brushed aside, and he assured us that there were no Germans about and that the innkeeper was friendly and had already agreed to accommodate us. With great trepidation, we accompanied him into the tiny inn. In short order, we had a mug of German beer. It tasted no better to us than the tepid English beer which we had previously found unexciting while flying out of our bases in England. Nevertheless, we drank it and pretended to like it but did not order a second mug.

As we waited for our food, the door opened, and our hearts sought the level of the floor as two German soldiers entered and sat down at a table across the room. You may think you can understand the word uncomfortable, but we added new dimensions to the meaning of the word. The soldiers, although they did not seem to be particularly interested in us, glanced frequently in our direction. This did absolutely nothing to calm our apprehension. Neither side in this quiet stand-off made any outward moves to indicate anything but idle curiosity, so we had nothing but a conversation-less, albeit hasty, lunch. We will never know whether the soldiers were curious about the presence of laborers who should have been laboring or whether or not they might have felt in jeopardy of being informed upon by someone who might question why they happened to be drinking beer while on duty. In either event, they quaffed a couple of mugs of beer, after which they paid their bill and left.

Our relief was intense! It became obvious to us that we, indeed, were not conspicuous and fitted into the landscape quite well, as long as we did not speak. This in no way alleviated our desire to remain out of the public eye, a practice we continued to maintain even more diligently.

One morning we awoke to the sound of distant thunder. We hoped, but could not be sure, that the sound was artillery. Our hopes were soon confirmed as each day the sounds drew closer, and they were quite sporadic, with no seeming relationship to the weather. Our original plan was still quite appropriate: stay holed up and let the fighting pass us. This would lessen the chance of being killed by either side making a mistake, as we attempted to cross the battle lines during the fighting. As the artillery sounds got closer and closer, we became more and more elated. Traffic in the village became heavier as people retreated ahead of the fighting.

On the second day of the obvious retreat, a horse-drawn wagon, full of the familiar blue gear of Luftwaffe origin, came rolling into view and stopped at the barn adjacent to our quarters. With this vehicle came a contingent of soldiers likewise sporting the blue of the Luftwaffe. It soon became obvious that they intended to stay in the barns of our complex. This was a rather disquieting turn of events and not at all to our liking. This theory became a reality when they unloaded their packs and other gear and placed them in the barn not fifty feet from where we were silently observing them.

The next day, the French went off to work, as usual. We naturally stayed inside, out of sight. Shortly thereafter, the German soldiers took their rifles and departed. They seemed to plan on returning since they left their goods in the barn with one soldier on duty to guard them. We continued to observe from our hideaway, and hours went by with no further activity. Nelson and I agreed that the guard on duty was none other than one of more friendly guards from our former camp. Since he was one of the less obnoxious guards, I discussed a plan with Nelson that had been forming in my mind. Here we were in the middle of a war and had absolutely nothing to show for it except a couple of German newspapers and some cigarette package labels. These would be poor pickings to show back home when we returned.

Accordingly, leaving Nelson as a backup in case I needed to be rescued, I went out slowly and "nonchalantly" approached the guard. He did not even lower his rifle from the sling over his shoulder. This was not because he recognized me but because I looked like any number of other nondescript itinerants who seemed constantly to be wandering around Germany. When I came close to him, I smiled, and in my best "Pidgin" German imitation I said, "For you der var iss offer." "Ya, Ya" was his reply as he still made no move to challenge me. He was an elderly man and seemed quite docile, and my courage improved immeasurably as I continued.

I was now close enough to overpower him if the need arose, before he could bring any hardware to bear on me. I told him that I was one of his "students" from good old Stalag Luft III. He then appeared to recognize me but still made no hostile moves. I told him that soon the Americans would be arriving and that he then would become a prisoner, to which he agreed. I said that I trusted him not to disclose my presence and that if, when capture became inevitable, he would give me his pistol as a souvenir, I would see to it that he received good treatment. To my surprise, he immediately unbuckled his holster belt and handed me the whole works, gun and ammunition as well. He then gave me his rifle and told me there were more in the barn, which I could have. I told him I did not want to arouse any suspicion with the other soldiers, and he should not say a word to anyone. He promised, and I returned to our quarters, where Nelson and I rejoiced at our good fortune. At least we felt a little more comfortable in having some means of defending ourselves if discovered by unfriendly Germans.

Our celebration was of short duration as a knock sounded at the door. We could think only that our guard had talked and that the Germans were here to pick us up. With pistol drawn, and Nelson backing me up with the rifle, I opened the door a crack. My heart skipped a beat. Sure enough there was a German soldier waiting! Seeing me, he made a reassuring gesture and held out his rifle and pistol for me to take. He wanted a promise of good treatment in return, just like the first guard. I took his weapons and assured him he also would receive good treatment. As before, I told him to keep our presence to himself, to which he agreed. A little later, another knock was heard, but this time there were two soldiers who, likewise, wanted to surrender. We were now assembling quite an arsenal and beginning to get a little nervous about all the attention we were attracting. We just wanted to be left alone.

In the meantime, the fighting sounded closer and closer, and even though it was only mid-afternoon, one by one, the Frenchmen began to return from the fields. They were becoming quite cocky now that the end of their incarceration seemed at hand. They became even more cocky as we began to arm them. Now a German emissary approached and said that the whole contingent wanted to surrender. We told them to come in single file, and with our armed group in presence, one by one, we accepted their weapons, keeping enough to arm the rest of the Frenchmen and disabling the rest of their pieces. We then herded all twenty-four of them into the barn, posting returned Frenchmen around the barn to keep them inside, on the threat of being instantly shot, if they so much as poked a head outside. I'm sure any of the Frenchmen, who had been imprisoned for three or four years, would gladly have complied with my order. It seemed the Frenchmen were unanimous in wanting me as their leader and would follow my instructions without question.

I became nervous about one thing missing. With this many soldiers, there had to be someone in command. We questioned the prisoners, and they disclosed the fact that there was indeed an officer and that he had his quarters in the adjacent farmhouse. Since this could be tricky, Nelson and I, accompanied by four armed Frenchmen, went to the farmhouse. Naturally, I was elected to enter. With the Frenchmen guarding the perimeter, and Nelson as my backup, I cautiously opened the front door, with my pistol drawn. I went slowly down the hall looking in each room with no success. I carefully opened the door at the end of the hall and could not believe my eyes. There, behind a beautiful mahogany desk stood an officer in his best uniform, saber at his side, medals on his chest, saluting me. He wanted to surrender formally. I relieved him of his side arms, so we could be sure negotiations were kept on a friendly basis, and called the Frenchmen to escort him to the barn with the same admonition under which the rest of the Germans were incarcerated.

That night, there was great rejoicing and camaraderie in our quarters, and no one came to lock us in. We posted guards around the barn where we had the Germans imprisoned and had a peaceful night's sleep. The next morning, there was an ominous silence. The artillery seemed to have taken a day off. Nothing new was happening. We had breakfast as usual and sat around doing mostly nothing. About mid-morning, we heard the sound of a vehicle approaching. Nelson and I went out to the street to have a look. Around the corner came a jeep. What a beautiful sight: an American jeep in camouflage colors, occupied by a Captain and a Sergeant both in battle dress. Both had automatic weapons, which they did not hesitate to hold with the business end in our direction. We signaled them to stop, which they did, keeping a very alert lookout about them as well as on us. We explained that we were escaped POWs and were interested in returning to Allied control as quickly as possible.

As we were talking, both suddenly leaped from the vehicle and took cover behind it with their guns pointing at the barn where we had the German prisoners. I asked what the problem was, and at that moment, I saw the answer as one of the German soldiers peeked around the corner of one of the doors. "There is a German soldier over there," said the Captain, keeping his rifle at the ready. I assured him that there were twenty-four and an officer in the barn and that they were harmless. He was not able to accept the "harmless" point of view, however, and told the Sergeant to get on the radio and call for help. Apparently this was a reconnaissance patrol and was somewhat ahead of the fighting forces. Within a short period of time, a half-track appeared, mounting two ominous looking fifty-caliber machine guns. The Germans were rousted out of the barn, searched, and lined up in a very familiar formation, with the half-track behind them pointing the fifties in a threatening attitude. In this manner, with their

The May 8, 1945 edition of "The Stars and Stripes" proclaims VE-Day has arrived!

The linemen celebrate VE-Day.

The officers celebrate VE-Day led by Lt. Millard Jenks who is taking his first drink.

Picadilly Circus goes crazy on VE-Day!

Lt. Frank Speer, top left, and new friends have a subdued celebration of VE-Day confined on board the hospital ship on the way to the States.

Winston Churchill threads his way through the exuberant crowd on his way to visit the American Embassy in London on VE-Day. (Konsler)

hands clasped behind their necks, we last saw the Germans heading up the road in the direction of the Allied forces. We were glad to be free of them and the threat they posed to our well-being.

A further discussion with the Captain concerning Nelson and me was not as fruitful as we would have liked it to have been. We were put on a truck and taken back towards our lines. We were fed well from ten-in-one rations, which were a new experience to us. It was then explained that until they received confirmation of our identities "through channels," we would be "detained." It was an extremely depressing moment for us when, after escaping, evading, and capturing a detachment of German soldiers and turning them over to the Allies, we continued to be prisoners, even though our captors were supposedly a friendly force. Having had previous experience with military channels, I envisioned months of freedom-less freedom while we were sorted out. We were subsequently locked in a German country schoolhouse, with a guard posted outside. The schoolhouse had a big teaching room with desks and blackboards and a separate quarters area where the schoolmaster lived. This was the section that appealed to us. It had a bed with a feather tick that must have been three feet thick. We lost no time in crawling into this scrumptious bed and, in less time than it takes to tell, we were completely oblivious to the world and the war.

Our luxury was short-lived; we were awakened as all Hell seemed to have broken loose. Tremendous explosions shook the earth and assaulted our ears. Flashes of light accompanied the explosions, and we soon determined that we were in the vicinity of a heavy artillery emplacement. It seemed that this might also become a good target, and we felt we did not want to continue to remain in the neighborhood where we could easily be killed by mistake. This was not our type of warfare, and we had no desire to be a part of it. Accordingly, we looked about for a means of escape. With all the noise and commotion, it was not too difficult to pry open a small rear window and squeeze through it to freedom. We headed up the road in the direction of the rear lines, keeping out of sight as much as possible, until we were a couple of miles from where we started. The traffic was rather heavy: trucks loaded with supplies heading south and trucks empty or carrying wounded heading north. We hitched a ride on a truck that was heading north, our favorite direction, until we reached the depot, the trucks' destination. There we chowed down and grabbed a little sleep. Here, as previously, in German-controlled Germany, no one seemed to care about inconspicuous people wandering around in the rear of the combat zone, and we moved about unchallenged.

We took the opportunity to do a little regular eating and sleeping for a couple of days. The food, by our standards, was outstanding. This was a feeling not shared by those who had become accustomed to ten-in-one rations over a long period of time. I felt, objectively, that they were a tremendous improvement over the "K" rations that had preceded them, and they offered a great variety not previously available. We did enjoy the meals, and we enjoyed the relief of not being on the run and fearful of every unusual sound. We were continually concerned by the fact that no one seemed to want to be responsible for finding out what to do with us. We soon felt that if anything was to be done, it was up to us to do it. We studied the traffic patterns and decided that everything seemed to be based in Nuremburg and that our best hope for repatriation lay in going there. We felt the rear echelon troops, not too busy with fighting the war, might be in the best position to figure out the solution to our problem.

The next day, we hitch-hiked a ride on a truck heading for Nuremburg. We arrived late in the day and spent the afternoon finding out that there was only one way out of the city heading back to France, and that was by air. We also determined who controlled the seating priorities of those heading back. Of course wounded, rightfully, had the top priority. Next were ranking officers and those on official business. Since we were none of the above, we fell into the last category of priorities, where the controller could show some personal discretion. Further inquiry disclosed his name and where he held "Court." We presented ourselves at his doorstep the following morning. After a morning of musical chairs, through a labyrinth of lesser officials, "the old Army game," moving ever closer to the door of this important man, we were finally ushered into his presence.

The controller was a Captain, who brusquely attempted to intimidate by shuffling "important" papers and pretending to not notice our entrance. Obviously, he was much too busy to attend to unimportant minor details. When he tired of his game, he asked us what we wanted. We gave him a brief résumé of our situation, to which he listened with seeming interest. He thought a while and then proclaimed that he had no precedent for this type of situation and gave us the now familiar line that he would have to inquire through channels regarding our disposition. Of course, we found this an unacceptable answer and kept pursuing alternative courses of action. During the ensuing conversation, he inquired about the contents of our packs, a question we had not previously been asked. He was dumbfounded when we opened our packs and showed him our arsenal of enemy weapons, pistols, daggers, insignia, and even an American flag. The flag, by the way, had been the property of the German officer we had captured; we had no idea of its intended purpose.

He immediately suggested that even if he were able to put us on a plane, he could not endanger the other passengers by allowing us on the plane with these weapons, since he had only our word for it that we were American ex-POWs. Blackmail, bribery, chicanery, whatever you may call it, the suggestions and its implications were immediately clear. Here sat an armchair-paddle-foot who had considerable control over our foreseeable future. Our needs superseded our pack-rat tendencies, and we unceremoniously rose to the occasion. I suggested that if possession of our armament were the only problem standing between us and our repatriation, we could certainly trust him to be custodian of our loot and, at some future time, he could forward the goods to us. Some more paper shuffling soon disclosed that he just happened to have a couple of seats available that afternoon on a plane going to camp Lucky Strike in France.

When we landed at Lucky Strike, we found an entirely different atmosphere. First, there was no way, short of desertion, to move any closer to home, other than through channels. However, they had a channel set up and operating. It was a great satisfaction to find that someone had considered the possibility of repatriates and done something about it. They were set up to handle repatriated POWs efficiently and with dispatch. The first step was a tent, where we were told to disrobe. Our clothes were then burned as we showered and were summarily deloused, with a powder sprayed on all hirsute areas of our naked bodies. We were given hospital robes and immediately admitted to the hospital, an old French chateau, surrounded by shell holes full of water. We were thoroughly examined, and treatment was prescribed. Since we were ambulatory, we were issued new uniforms and allowed to roam somewhat at will. We were put on strict diets because of our malnutrition-orientated ailments and watched very closely as we adapted to our treatment. With our lice gone, our scabies or scurvy and our digestive system problems became the focus of our medical attention. The results were good, and it took only about a week until we were again on our way; not that we were cured, but at least we were not infectious and not required to be confined to bed. We did, however, require continuous daily monitoring.

The first day or two, in the hospital, was somewhat of a disappointment in that we were placed on a very strict diet, a sudden change from our recent days of full stomachs. By now, we had become consummate scroungers and accepted the challenge in spite of the dread consequences of continued overeating. The second night in the hospital, we decided to make a food run. We left our room after lights-out and made our way to the supply tent behind the hospital. There our plans went awry. As we neared the tent, Nelson, in the very poor light of blackout conditions, had the misfortune of stepping too close to the slippery bank of a shell hole and fell in. He was up to his neck in muddy water, and the noise of my laughter and the tug-of-war aspect of pulling him out of the hole aroused the guard and cut short our planned sortie. The guard, who was really the custodian of the supplies, did take pity on our plight and invited us in to dry off in front of his heater while he treated us to some cookies and coffee.

On the way back to our room, I decided to stop at the latrine, which was outside the chateau. On the way in, I encountered a nurse, who had been involved with our hospitalization, as she was coming out of the women's side of the latrine/wash-house, carrying her helmet in hand. It was obvious she had taken her helmet full of water in with her to wash her hair because it was as wet as her hair. She asked how I had become so messed up with mud. I told her of our little foray, and she said that since we had been eating so well since our escape, she saw no reason to have us on such limited diets, and that I could join her in the nurses' mess if I chose. I mentioned my buddy Nelson, and she somewhat reluctantly agreed to include him in the invitation. From then on, we ate our meals in the nurses' mess, and a welcome change it was.

One day, near the end of our stay in the hospital, she mentioned that there was a good movie playing that night in the camp theater and that she would gladly take me with her if I were so inclined. The hospital was boring, to say the least, after all the episodes we had been through in recent months, so it sounded like a good idea, and I agreed to go with her. The movie was quite enjoyable, and we headed back towards the chateau a block away on the dimly-lit street. She walked rather close and bumped my arm a couple of times in a very suggestive manner. I tried to ignore what appeared to be an invitation, but the invitation became much more open and required an answer. I told her I was happily married and was not inclined to stray. She suggested that I had been away a long time and no one would ever know the difference. I said that I would know, but this did not prove to be a satisfactory answer. I then changed tactics and said that in any event, probably as the result of my long imprisonment and malnutrition, I had no sexual feelings whatsoever but thanks for the consideration. I had to bite my tongue for telling such a terrible lie, but I preferred to keep it that way. I often wondered if that went on my medical record, and if, in fact, it were not some medical questionnaire type of query given to all returning POWs. But again, maybe she felt sorry for me in my long abstinence, and felt she was doing her patriotic duty in offering to help in any way she could. I will never know.

The next day we received some back-pay and orders to ship out. We were flown to a port, where we boarded a hospital ship. Here we were unquestionably captives again, but we had something definite to look forward to, and the time did not drag. A couple of days later, we ended up in a harbor in Wales. No amount of pleading, bargaining, or cajoling was successful in getting us off that boat for even an instant, let alone long enough to visit my Group at Debden. It probably was just as well, because most of our Group had been dispersed to other bases or was on the way home. Also, this way I will never know who wound up with some of my treasures, which somehow never managed to get shipped to my wife when I was shot down.

The next day, the most unusual thing happened. A group of us, Nelson and I and a couple of nurses and three or four doctors, were sitting at a table on the deck. We had each ordered a drink and were conversing as we looked out over the town and watched the preparations being made for our imminent departure. Our conversation was interrupted by a loudspeaker announcement that the word we had all been awaiting for so long was now a fact. They announced that the Germans had surrendered, unconditionally. We were awestruck, but it soon sank in that this was in fact true, and the loudspeaker soon repeated the confirmation of our hopes.

The timing could not have been more perfect!

We raised our glasses, clinked them together and toasted the end of the war in Europe, as the ship slowly pulled away from the dock and headed for home.

ABOUT THE AUTHOR

Frank Speer was born in Pittsburg, Pennsylvania. Raised on a farm in southeastern part of the state, he graduated from Allentown High School; and later married his high-school sweetheart, one month before the Japanese attack on Pearl Harbor.

Frank was very patriotic and had a passion to fly. He consequently enlisted in the Army Air Corps and graduated from Aviation Cadets in 1943. He was assigned to the Fourth Fighter Group where he flew in combat over Europe in P-51 Mustangs. He soon became an Ace, was awarded the Distinguished Flying Cross, the Air Medal with three Oak Leaf Clusters and the Distinguished Unit Citation. Subsequently he was shot down by flak and became a Prisoner-of-War. Eventually, he escaped and was repatriated.

After a tour in South America, Frank was discharged and became a member of the Air Force Reserve. He worked as an engineer for the Bell Telephone Co. and later started his own business. After retiring, he became a real estate agent, and began to write. His wife and five children encouraged him to write of his wartime experiences. His published books are: Wingman, The Debden Warbirds and One Down, One Dead.

GLOSSARY

ABORT – Turn back

CHATTANOOGA – Railroad strafing mission

E/A – Enemy Aircraft

IFF – Identification Friend or Foe radar

JACKPOT – Airdrome strafing mission

KIA – Killed in action

MIA – Missing in action

OPS – Operations office

OTU – Operations Training Unit

POW – Prisoner of War

PRANG – Crash

RAMROD – Bomber escort mission

RHUBARB – Low level strafing mission

ROADSTEAD – Attack ships or ports mission

RODEO – Bomber escort mission using bombers as bait

SHOW – Slang for a mission

VERBOTTEN – Forbidden (German)

Caption for rear cover picture:

Memorial dedicated to 128 Fourth Fighter Group pilots
Killed in action in WWII—Dayton Air Force Museum – Ohio

INDEX

Acknowledgment	7
Prolog Aviation Cadets	11
Chapter I The Lust for Acceptance	25
Chapter II The Squadron Commander	37
Chapter III The Mission Continues	55
Chapter IV We Sight the Enemy	64
Chapter V 24 May-Mission Berlin	92
Chapter VI The Last Mission	121
Chapter VII For You the War is Over	132
Chapter VIII Welcome to Stalag Luft III	148
Chapter IX The Endless March	175
Chapter X Our New Home-Stalag 17D	187
Chapter XI C'est Fini	203
Glossary	221

CPSIA information can be obtained at www.ICGtesting.com
Printed in the USA
LVOW12s2203300114
371755LV00001B/109/P